T...

Vegetables

Taylor's Pocket Guide to

Vegetables

ANN REILLY
Consulting Editor

A Chanticleer Press Edition

Houghton Mifflin Company

Boston

For information about
permission to reproduce selections from this book,
write to Permissions,
Houghton Mifflin Company, 2 Park Street,
Boston, Massachusetts 02108

Based on Taylor's Encyclopedia of Gardening, Fourth Edition,
Copyright © 1961 by Norman Taylor,
revised and edited by
Gordon P. DeWolf, Jr.

Prepared and produced by Chanticleer Press, New York
Typeset by Dix Type, Inc., Syracuse, New York
Printed and bound by
Dai Nippon, Tokyo, Japan

Library of Congress Catalog Card Number: 89-85026
ISBN: 0-395-52245-5

DNP   10   9   8   7   6   5   4   3   2   1

CONTENTS

Introduction
GARDENING WITH VEGETABLES
6

The Plant Descriptions
VEGETABLES
25

Appendices
FROST DATE MAP
106

GARDEN PESTS AND DISEASES
108

ALTERNATIVE GARDENING METHODS
112

VEGETABLE VARIETIES
114

GLOSSARY
117

PHOTO CREDITS
123

INDEX
124

GARDENING WITH VEGETABLES

GROWING VEGETABLES is in many ways the most rewarding kind of gardening. What could be better than harvesting the ripe fruits of your labor just steps from the kitchen and sharing them in delicious, healthful meals with your family and friends? There are hundreds of types of vegetables to grow in any garden, large or small. All it takes is a bit of knowledge and some tender loving care. Within a few months after planting, your crops will be ready to pick and enjoy.

What Is a Vegetable?

Vegetables are usually herbaceous (not woody) plants grown for food. Depending on the crop, the leaves, leafstalks, fruits, roots, or flower buds may be eaten. There is some overlap between vegetables and such fruits as melons and strawberries, but for this book we have chosen not to make distinctions. We include vegetables and a few fruits that are easy and rewarding to grow in the home garden.

Vegetables are classified as annuals, biennials, or perennials, depending on their life cycle. Most vegetables are true annuals or are grown as annuals, which means they grow, flower, set their fruit, and die within one growing year. Annuals are usually further classified by their hardiness—that is, their ability to withstand cold. Tender annuals will not tolerate frost or, usually, cold weather; they are planted in spring after frost danger has passed. Half-hardy vegetables will grow when weather is cool but will not tolerate heavy frost. Hardy vegetables will tolerate frost and can be planted in the garden in early spring or grown in fall.

Vegetables are sometimes designated as "warm-season" or "cool-season." Warm-season vegetables are the tender ones that grow best during the heat of summer. Cool-season vegetables are half-hardy or hardy and grow best during the cooler days of spring, fall, and even winter in mild areas.

Biennials grow into sizable plants during their first year but do not flower, set fruit, and die until the second year. Biennial vegetables that are grown for their leaves or their roots are often grown as annuals, because the leaves and roots may be tough or bitter the second year. There are a few vegetables that are true perennials—they die to the ground each fall after harvest and return each spring, to grow and produce anew. Many tender perennials are grown as annuals in areas where winter cold would kill them.

First Steps

Selecting the right site for your vegetable garden involves both common sense and a few scientific factors. No matter where you live—country, city, or suburb—you can grow vegetables successfully if you learn just a few basics.

Sunlight Requirements

Most vegetables must be grown in full sun, which means at least six hours of direct sun each day. You should plant early-spring vegetables and warm-season crops in the areas of your garden that receive the most sun. Sites that receive less light can still produce some tasty vegetables; for example, leafy vegetables will grow well where there is shade in the afternoon. In very hot climates, most vegetables actually benefit from some shade during the hottest part of the day. In laying out your garden, consider the amount and intensity of sunlight it will receive throughout the day. Take into account not only shade, but also the average cloud cover, fog, smog, and hours of daylight in your area. (Midsummer days are longer in northern latitudes than in the South, so many vegetables will grow faster and larger in the North.)

Other Factors

Sunlight isn't the only factor to consider when you are choosing a site for your vegetable garden. The location should have adequate air circulation and good drainage, and it should be far away from large trees and shrubs, whose roots will compete for water and food. You may have to put up a fence or other protective device to ward off wildlife.

Garden Soil

Vegetables grow best in healthy soil that drains moderately quickly, retains nutrients, and contains a fair amount of organic matter. Regardless of its present condition, your soil will probably require some modification to bring its quality to a level where vegetables will thrive. Generally this means incorporating more organic matter and nutrients.

If your soil is clay—meaning that it bakes hard, sheds water, drains slowly, and is slow to warm up in spring—correct it by incorporating organic matter and sand, or build raised beds and fill them with improved soil. Adding gypsum (calcium sulfate), which improves drainage and aeration, will also help. If you have sandy soil, which warms up quickly in spring but drains and dries out rapidly, use large amounts of organic matter to prepare it for vegetable gardening.

Organic Matter

Organic matter in soil helps water penetrate, stores nutrients, activates beneficial soil bacteria, and improves drainage. There are many types of organic matter you can work into your soil: peat moss, leaf mold, dried manure, treated sewage sludge, or compost.

Many vegetable gardeners make their own compost so they always have a large supply of organic matter. You can build a pile in an out-of-the-way corner of the garden; enclose it in chicken wire if you like, or purchase a compost bin. To mix compost, use a formula of two to three parts green matter, one part dried matter, and one part garden soil. The green matter can be kitchen or garden waste that has not been treated with harmful chemicals (grass clippings and other plant remains should be fermented in a plastic bag for two or three weeks before being added to the pile). The dried matter can be chopped leaves. Layer the ingredients and wet the pile. Turn as needed when decomposition begins, especially if the pile is generating excessive heat, and use the compost when it is brown and crumbly. Once a pile is "working," save some of the compost to work into next year's pile to speed up the decomposition process.

The Importance of pH

The acidity or alkalinity of a soil is called its "pH" and is measured on a scale of 1 to 14. A pH of 7 is neutral; below 7 is increasingly acid and above 7 is increasingly alkaline. If you are not sure of the pH of your soil, don't guess. You can buy a soil test kit at your local garden supply store or take a sample and have it tested by your Cooperative Extension Service or a soil testing lab. If you live in the East or Northwest, your soil is probably acid; if you live in the Midwest or Southwest, it is most likely alkaline.

Most vegetables prefer a very slightly acid to neutral soil, with a pH of 6 to 7. Exceptions are noted in the individual plant descriptions. If your soil is too acid, you can raise the pH by adding lime. Dolomitic limestone is recommended; it is slow acting, does not burn plant roots, and contains the essential elements magnesium and calcium. To lower the pH of your soil, add sulfur. Organic matter (especially peat moss) and many fertilizers are acid and will lower pH.

Fertilizer

Complete fertilizers contain nitrogen, phosphorus, and potassium (potash); the formulas on the label, such as 5–10–5 or 10–10–10, indicate the proportions of these elements. The first number is the percentage of nitrogen; the second, phosphate; the third, potash.

Vegetables do need to be fertilized, but controlling types and amounts of fertilizer can be tricky. With too little, plants may turn yellow and not grow. With too much, fruiting vegetables will produce many leaves but few flowers or fruits. As a guideline, use a fertilizer relatively high in nitrogen (one with a 20–10–10 rating, for example) for leafy vegetables and one high in phosphorus for others; apply it according to the label directions and the plant descriptions herein. Make adjustments if your plants are not growing as they should.

Many soils are deficient in phosphorus, which moves very slowly through the soil to plant roots. When preparing a new bed, it is a good idea to incorporate a high-phosphorus fertilizer (such as superphosphate: 0–46–0) so there will be a good supply of it for many years.

Getting Started

Every vegetable gardener's goal is to grow the largest number of vegetables possible in the space available with the least amount of maintenance. An important step in achieving this goal is careful planning.

Planning the Garden

Before you do any actual work in your vegetable garden, it is a good idea to plan it out on paper. This way you can experiment with different sizes and shapes before choosing your final plan. It is easiest to plan and maintain a garden that is planted in rows or blocks. Lay out your plants so that the taller ones will not block access to the shorter ones. If you live in the North, try to place tall plants and structures on the east side so they do not shade the garden in the afternoon.

One of the easiest ways to decide what to plant in your garden is to make a list of the vegetables that you would like to grow (and that are hardy in your area) and then label each by its season: spring, summer, or fall. Season is determined by whether the plants are cool- or warm-season vegetables and the number of days they require to maturity. The days-to-maturity number, given on seed packets and in the plant descriptions in this book, is an indication of how much growing time the plant will need before it can be harvested. Experience will tell you that you'll need about two-thirds of your space for warm-weather crops. After you harvest your spring crops, you can plant a late warm-season crop or hold the space open for a fall crop.

From the size of your garden plan (if you are a beginner, you shouldn't start with anything larger than 15 by 20 feet) and from the information given in the plant descriptions about spacing, you can determine how many plants to grow or buy. Keep records so you can make adjustments in following years.

Buying Plants and Seeds

Your vegetable garden will be most successful if you select the right varieties for your area—those that have been proven to thrive in your climate, soil, and growing season, and to resist diseases prevalent in your region. Your county Cooperative Extension Service publishes a list of the varieties that do best in your area. Seed catalogs often give this information as well. You may also want to experiment with some of the many new varieties available every year.

There are both hybrid and nonhybrid (called "open-pollinated") varieties of many vegetables. The hybrids are usually bred to be more vigorous, offering greater yield and increased disease resistance. When buying vegetable plants or seeds, especially tomatoes, look for initials after the variety name, which indicate resistance to one or more diseases (Roma VF plum tomato, for example, is resistant to verticillium root rot and fusarium wilt).

You can buy seeds from mail-order companies and garden supply and hardware stores. Mail-order companies usually have better selections, and you can order specific varieties from them that may not be available in stores. Seed packets are imprinted with an expiration date; never buy outdated seeds. Buy seeds early for the best selection and store them in a cool, dry place.

If you buy plants instead of seeds, look for healthy, green plants, with no signs of insects or diseases, that obviously have been watered and well tended. If you can't plant them right away, keep the pots or flats in a protected spot and check them every day to see if they need water.

Preparing the Site

After choosing where to plant your garden, skim off the top 1 to 2 inches of soil or grass to remove everything that is growing there, as well as ungerminated weed seeds. The material you removed can be composted. If the plot contains deep-rooted grasses or weeds, apply an herbicide to kill them before preparing the soil. Be sure to use an herbicide that is not residual in the soil (read labels carefully); you should be able to plant within a week or so of using the herbicide.

Before you start to prepare your garden, be sure that the soil is not too wet to be worked, or you will compact and ruin it. Take a handful of soil and squeeze it. If it remains solid and sticky, it is too wet; wait a few days and try again. If it crumbles easily, it can be worked. If it is dry or dusty, water it deeply several days before working it. You can prepare soil in the fall if you will be planting early the next spring.

Spread 2 to 3 inches of organic matter over the soil surface, along with lime if the pH needs to be raised, fertilizer, and any other soil amendments that are necessary. Spade the area to a depth of 8 to 12 inches (you can rent or buy a Rototiller to make the work easier). Rake the area level, and you are ready to plant. If your garden is large, you should excavate soil to make aisles, piling this soil into the planting rows to raise them somewhat and improve drainage.

If you are preparing the soil in an existing garden, add about 1 inch of organic matter (unless the garden did not grow well the previous year, in which case you should prepare it as if it were a new bed), fertilizer, and any other soil amendments as needed. Some gardeners plant a "green manure" crop in the fall, which is a crop of grasses or legumes that grows over winter and is incorporated into the soil the following spring.

Planting the Garden

Climate is a major factor in determining when to put plants and seeds in the garden. Refer to the frost date map on pages 106–107, which divides the country into seven areas according to length of growing season and prevailing climate during the growing season. The dates given are the approximate dates of the last frost, and the numbers of days indicate the average length of the growing season—that is, the number of frost-free days. It is a good idea to check this information with your county Cooperative Extension Service; your proximity to a body of water, ridge, valley, or city could affect your frost-free dates.

Now consider the hardiness of the plants you are growing. Tender annuals cannot be planted until after the last frost date, when the soil is warm. Plant half-hardy annuals two to four weeks before and hardy annuals one to two months before the last spring frost. If you are planting annuals for a fall crop, subtract the number of days to maturity (indicated on the seed packet) from the total number of days in the growing season in your region to determine when in the summer or fall the vegetable must be planted. Most biennials and perennials can be planted in spring; check the individual plant descriptions for exact instructions.

Starting Seeds Indoors

The seeds of some vegetables can be sown directly into the garden, but others must be started in a controlled environment or given a head start because the plants need a long time to mature. You can buy seedlings of these vegetables or start the seeds yourself indoors. Check the individual plant descriptions for specific guidelines, but in general, seeds should be started indoors six to eight weeks before outdoor planting.

To start seeds indoors, you will need containers; you can purchase them or make them from milk cartons or aluminum baking tins. They should be 2½ to 4 inches deep and have drainage holes. Wash plastic or metal containers in a 10 percent solution of household bleach and rinse them in water before using them. You can also use special containers such as peat pots or Jiffy 7s, which are compressed peat encased in mesh. Peat or fiber containers must never be reused for sowing seeds; their sterility cannot be assured. Use individual containers for growing vegetables that do not transplant well, so the transplanting shock will be less severe.

Sow seeds in a soilless mix of 50 percent peat moss and 50 percent perlite or vermiculite (never sow seeds in garden soil, and do not reuse sowing mediums). You can purchase sowing medium or mix your own. Fill the container to within ¼ inch of the top with pre-moistened medium. Sow the seeds following the packet directions and cover the container with a clear plastic bag or a pane of glass until the seeds germinate. The container should not need watering during this time. Place it in good light but not direct sun.

Most seeds germinate best if the air temperature is 68° to 72° F, and if the temperature of the medium is a little warmer. You can achieve this with heating cables, which you can buy from seed catalogs or at a garden supply store, or by placing the containers in a warm spot, such as on top of the refrigerator. After the seeds have germinated, the bottom heat is no longer necessary and the flats should be moved into full sun or under fluorescent lights.

Many young seedlings are killed by a disease called "damping off," which causes them to topple over and die. To prevent damping off, use soilless medium, drench the seed flats with a fungicide such as benomyl prior to sowing, and do not over-water the seedlings.

Once the seeds have germinated, water as soon as the medium starts to dry out. Water from the bottom, or use a very fine spray of water from a rubber-bulb syringe to prevent dislodging the small seedlings. When they are at least 1 inch high and have four leaves, you can transplant the seedlings into individual cells or containers. This will make the transition into the garden easier later on. Hold off on fertilizing for two weeks after transplanting. If you choose not to transplant seedlings to individual pots, thin them to about 1 inch apart when they have developed two sets of true leaves. Start fertilizing weekly with quarter-strength, soluble plant food.

Place the seedlings on a sunny windowsill or under fluorescent lights. Keep the lights 6 inches above the tops of the seedlings and leave them on for 12 to 14 hours each day. Fluorescent lights generally give better and more uniform results than a sunny windowsill.

One week before it is time to plant your vegetable seedlings into the garden, start a process called "hardening off," which gradually acclimatizes the young plants to the outdoors. On the first day, move the plants outside to a shaded and protected spot and bring them back inside again that night. Each day, increase the length of time the plants are outdoors and the amount of light they receive. By the end of the week, your vegetable plants will be ready to go in the garden. Seedlings can also be hardened off in a cold frame, which is a bottomless box set on the ground with a removable glass or clear plastic top. The sun will enter through the top, while the box itself protects seedlings from cold and wind. You can buy a cold frame or make one from wood and an old window.

Sowing Seeds Outdoors

The seeds of vegetables that have a short maturity time, as well as those that do not transplant well, should be sown directly in the garden. Rake the prepared soil level and moisten it lightly before sowing. Make slight furrows with the edge of your trowel and sow the seeds into the furrows, following the directions in the plant descriptions regarding planting depth and spacing. If you sow the seeds in rows, the garden will be easier to work, and you will be better able to distinguish between vegetable and weed seedlings.

Keep the soil evenly moist at all times until the seeds have germinated. After that, water them daily until they have four to six leaves and then gradually reduce watering to about once a week. When the plants are several inches high, thin them to the degree indicated in each plant description. Moisten the soil before thinning and be careful not to disturb the roots of the plants that remain. Thinnings of greens can be cooked; some can be transplanted.

Planting the Vegetables

Whether you buy vegetable plants or start your own indoors from seeds, the method of planting is the same. To reduce transplanting shock, plant on a cloudy day or in the afternoon. Water the prepared site and the plants well. Carefully remove the plants from their containers; be sure to keep the root ball intact to avoid root damage. Push up from the bottom of the container or turn the container upside down and rap the bottom if necessary to dislodge the plant, but never pull plants out by their stems. If the seedlings were grown in peat pots, peel away as much of the pot as possible and, when you plant, be sure that the rim is below the soil surface.

Dig a hole slightly larger than the root ball, set the plant into the ground at the same level at which it was growing, and carefully firm the soil around the roots. If the roots encircle the root ball tightly, loosen them before planting. Water well after planting and again daily until you see new growth.

Protecting New Plants

Until they are large and strong, young seedlings are subject to some devastating effects of nature. If a late frost threatens and you have already planted your warm-season vegetables, cover them with plastic film, plastic milk jugs with the bottoms cut out, or cloches (transparent plant covers). It doesn't matter what you use, as long as it protects the plants from frost damage. When the weather warms up again, remove the protection.

Be on the lookout for snails and slugs, and apply bait to stop them. Cutworms often eat vegetable stems at soil level; place a protective collar around the plants to keep them away. Keep birds away from seedlings by covering beds with fine chicken wire until plants are large. Rodents and rabbits can be discouraged with fences or traps.

Maintaining the Vegetable Garden

There is no such thing as a maintenance-free vegetable garden, but performing just a few basic chores will keep your garden productive. Visit your garden at least once a day to observe its progress and to watch for any problems.

Watering and Fertilizing

Water vegetables deeply but infrequently to encourage a strong root system that will tolerate summer heat and adverse conditions. Too frequent watering encourages shallow roots, which are ill equipped to combat heat, drought, and winds. If it does not rain, apply 1 to 2 inches of water once a week unless it is very hot or windy, in which case you will need to water more frequently. Keep plant foliage as dry as possible when you water. Soaker hoses are good for this; they also use less water. If you water overhead, do it in the morning so the foliage is dry before dark (wet foliage attracts disease).

Fertilize your vegetables as instructed in the individual plant descriptions. Be sure to use the right fertilizers for each crop. If you notice that your vegetables are producing lush foliage but no fruits or flowers, stop fertilizing immediately.

Mulching and Weeding

A mulch is a protective covering spread over the ground and around plants to keep weeds from germinating, conserve moisture, and keep the soil (and roots) at an even temperature. If you are growing cool-season vegetables, apply a mulch early in spring to keep the soil cool. If you are growing warm-season vegetables, do not apply mulch until the soil is warm and the plants are growing, because the mulch will keep the soil cool and deter growth if put down too early.

Organic mulches, such as peat moss, bark chips, dried grass clippings, and straw, are beneficial because they break down into humus and enrich the soil. Plastic mulch is a favorite in vegetable gardens; be sure to cut holes in the plastic so water and nutrients can go through. Clear plastic traps more heat than black plastic; it is a good mulch to use if you are growing warm-season vegetables in the North. There is a new inorganic mulch made of woven fabric called landscape cloth; it holds down weeds but allows water to pass through easily.

Weeds compete with vegetables for space, food, and water, and often harbor insects and diseases. Even if you mulch, a few weeds will probably get through. They should be removed as soon as they appear; this is easiest to do when the soil is wet. In large gardens, you can do your weeding with a hoe.

Winter Cleanup

Throughout the season you should pull up each crop after it has stopped producing. Before the ground freezes in late fall, remove everything from the garden except for perennials and, in mild areas, any crops you are planning to harvest the following spring. If the plants are free of disease, throw them in the compost pile. You are then free to spend the winter browsing through seed catalogs and planning next season's garden.

Harvesting and Storing Vegetables

The harvesting times for individual vegetables are given in the plant descriptions. It is important to harvest vegetables as soon as they are ready, not only because they are most flavorful when they are ripe, but to keep the plants producing.

Harvest most vegetables in the early morning when they are still cool (beans are the exception; pick them after the dew has dried). Bring along a bucket of cold water and plunge the vegetables into the water as soon as you pick them. Change the water and repeat the dunking two or three times, then refrigerate (do not refrigerate okra). This method keeps many vegetables sweet.

Once you have harvested and eaten your fill, it is up to you how to use the rest of your crop. You may want to share the bounty with friends and neighbors, or you may want to preserve some of the harvest to enjoy over the winter.

You can store root vegetables and most winter squashes in a cool, dark, dry place. Many other vegetables can be canned or frozen (some should be blanched first), and a number can be pickled. A good basic cookbook can tell you how to preserve most fresh vegetables.

A Note on Plant Names

Like all plants vegetables have a common, or English, name and a scientific, or Latin, name. Asparagus, Brussels sprouts, and zucchini are all common names. Occasionally, a vegetable has more than one common name; garbanzo bean and chick pea are both names for the same plant.

Scientific names, which are standard worldwide, always have two parts. The first part is called the generic name; it tells us to which genus (plural, genera) a plant belongs. The second part of the name tells us the species. (A species is a kind of plant or animal that is capable of reproducing with members of its own kind, but is genetically isolated from others. *Homo sapiens* is a species.) Most genera have many species; *Brassica,* a genus in this book, has more than 40 species, one of which is *Brassica oleracea,* wild cabbage.

Under intense development, species have given rise to groups of agricultural forms that produce the products we think of as vegetables. Thus *Brassica oleracea,* wild cabbage, has been developed in several different ways; the resulting groups are familiar to us as vegetables. Broccoli is *Brassica oleracea,* Botrytis Group; Brussels sprouts are really *B. oleracea,* Gemmifera Group; and cabbage is *B. oleracea,* Capitata Group. Fortunately for gardeners, it is not necessary to memorize these names in order to grow vegetables, for most are sold under their familiar "table" names.

Many vegetable groups are then further broken down into varieties or cultivars. A variety is a group or class of plants occurring naturally within a species, with traits that distinguish it from the typical form and from other varieties within the same species. A cultivar (short for cultivated variety) is a man-made variety; that is, a variety created by a plant breeder. The term variety is often used to refer to both varieties and cultivars. The names of varieties and cultivars are usually added to the scientific name; they may be written in italics, or in roman type and surrounded by single quotation marks. *Daucus carota* is the scientific name for Queen Anne's Lace (also known as wild carrot); *Daucus carota* var. *sativus* is the name for the carrot cultivated in the garden.

A hybrid is a plant that is the result of a cross between two genera, two species, two varieties, or two cultivars. Hybrids are often indicated by an × within the scientific name. *Fragaria* × *ananassa,* strawberry, is a hybrid in this book.

Organization of the Plant Accounts

The plant accounts in this book are arranged alphabetically by common name. All of the large groups, such as beans, squashes, and melons, have been left intact, so you will find lima bean under "bean," zucchini under "squash," and watermelon under "melon." The individual accounts deal with each vegetable in its typical form. Some of the photos show varieties, hybrids, or cultivars; those are named in the text.

The number of days in the upper right corner of each account indicates the days to maturity—the number of days required from seed germination to harvest.

One Last Word

Whether you're a beginner growing one of the vegetable-garden classics or an experienced gardener looking to try new foods, whether you garden in the country, suburbs, or surrounded by asphalt, this book offers special pointers for growing a wide variety of vegetables. Your gardening efforts will be rewarded with the pleasure of tasting food grown with your own skill, fresh from your garden.

Vegetables

Artichoke *(Cynara scolymus)*

Artichokes are the large, imma-ture flower buds of a dark sil-very green plant that grows to 5 feet high. Artichokes are perennial in mild climates; in colder areas, they must be grown as annuals. They re-quire a long, cool growing season and do best in California. In the North they can be raised only from root divisions started indoors during midwinter.

GROWING TIPS

For best results, plant 1 root each in 3-gallon containers and grow them indoors until the last spring frost. Transplant them to a sunny site, spacing the plants 4 feet apart. They grow best in fertile, sandy, well-drained soil. Water artichokes fre-quently during dry spells; fertilize at planting time and again when plants are 2 feet tall. Apply a mulch but be on the lookout for snails and slugs. Harvest in fall to midwinter when buds are about 4 inches across; cut the stems 3–4 inches below the bud with a sharp knife.

Arugula *(Eruca vesicaria sativa)*

Also known as rocket or roquette, arugula is a sturdy, cold-tolerant leafy vegetable. It has deeply toothed leaves that can be cooked or used as salad greens. Its strong aroma and flavor are reminiscent of peanuts.

GROWING TIPS

Plant arugula seeds thickly, ¼ inch deep, in rows or wide bands in early spring and again in late summer. Fall sowings are possible in the South. Avoid planting in summer; short summer nights force plants to flower and go to seed before sufficient vegetative growth has taken place. To harvest, shear off whole plants 2–3 inches above soil level, leaving the central leaf buds for further growth, or snap off only the outer leaves.

Asparagus *(Asparagus officinalis)*

2 Years

Asparagus is a perennial vegetable that sends up edible stalks in spring. The scales at the top and along the length of the stalks are leaf buds that produce feathery foliage on unharvested spears. Asparagus is extremely difficult to grow in very hot, humid regions.

GROWING TIPS

Asparagus can be grown from seeds or from root divisions called crowns. To build up a strong root system, do not harvest plants during the first 2 years. Plant asparagus in late spring in most parts of the country; in the mid-South, plant in fall or winter. Set the crowns 15 inches apart in deeply prepared, rich, well-drained soil that is high in phosphorus. Fertilize every spring and fall. Cut spears when they are 5–7 inches long, taking care not to damage the roots. Harvest for 4 weeks only; after that, allow foliage to grow.

Broad Bean *(Vicia faba)*

Broad beans, also known as fava beans, grow on erect, 5-foot plants that have thick, succulent stems. The pods may grow 6–12 inches long; the edible seeds are embedded in a white, woolly lining. Some people are allergic to the mature seeds of broad beans; try a few before planting if you've never eaten them before.

GROWING TIPS

Broad beans need cool, relatively frost-free weather to produce at their best. Plant seeds in early spring in full sun and well-drained soil. Set them 1 inch deep and 8–10 inches apart in rows 3–4 feet apart. Provide a trellis or other support. Mulch seedlings with straw or pine needles. When the beans are half-grown, you can cook and eat the entire pod like snap beans. Shell older pods like peas and mix the seeds with cut-up pods.

Lima Bean *(Phaseolus limensis)*

Lima beans are flat, kidney-shaped beans that have a mealy or nut-like flavor. There are pole and bush varieties; the pole varieties mature later but bear for a longer period of time. The bush variety Fordhook 242 is pictured here.

Growing Tips

Sow lima bean seeds in spring after all danger of frost has passed and the soil is warm. Set them 2–3 inches apart, 1 inch deep in clay soils and 1½ inches deep in sandy soils. They need full sun and good drainage. Incorporate fertilizer into the soil before planting but do not fertilize again. Thin plants to 6–8 inches apart and stake the pole varieties. Pick the beans when the pods are 3–5 inches long and shell them before cooking.

Snap Bean *(Phaseolus vulgaris)*

50–70 Days

Snap beans, or string beans, which may be green, yellow, or purple, grow 5–12 inches long. Pole varieties mature somewhat later than bush varieties but usually produce beans over a longer period of time. Bush beans are more heat resistant, but neither grows well in extreme heat. The pole variety Blue Lake is pictured.

GROWING TIPS

Plant seeds outdoors in well-drained soil after the last spring frost; fertilize once, at planting time. Where summers are short and soil is too cool for proper germination, start seeds indoors in peat pots and move the seedlings outdoors after frost. Plant seeds for bush varieties 2 inches apart in rows 2 feet apart or in bands 6–12 inches wide. Thin seedlings to 3–4 inches apart. For pole beans, plant 2 or 3 seeds per pole; thin to the strongest seedling. Harvest beans when they are large enough to eat.

Beet *(Beta vulgaris, Crassa Group)*

Beets are grown for their sweet-flavored, edible roots, which may be purple, red, yellow, or white. The reddish-green leaves of garden beets are also edible. Beets are usually winter hardy but do not taste as good the second year.

Growing Tips

Beets are moderately frost resistant and do not grow well in very hot, dry weather. They like rich, loose, well-drained soil with a neutral pH. Add fertilizer before sowing; no further feeding is necessary. Plant seed outdoors 2–3 weeks before the last spring frost. Sow them 2 inches apart and ¼–½ inch deep. Thin seedlings to 3–4 inches apart (use the thinnings for soup greens). Do not try to transplant beets; they usually develop root deformities if you do. For a continuous supply, sow seeds every 3 weeks until months before the first fall frost. Pull mature beets from the ground when they are 2–3 inches across.

Broccoli *(Brassica oleracea,* Botrytis Group)   70–95 Days

The parts of broccoli that we eat are the fleshy stems and central heads of densely clustered, immature flower buds. The variety shown here is Early Emerald.

GROWING TIPS

Broccoli needs a long, cool growing season. Start seeds indoors or purchase plants and set them outside several weeks before the last spring frost. Space plants 18–24 inches apart in rows 2½–3 feet apart. For a fall crop, set plants into the garden in early to late summer. Broccoli grows best in rich, moist, well-drained soil. Fertilize prior to planting and again when plants are 6–8 inches high, 12–15 inches high, and when buds form. Water the plants well and mulch to keep the ground moist and cool. Cut the central stem before the yellow flowers show. Side branches may continue to produce heads.

Brussels Sprouts
(*Brassica oleracea*, Gemmifera Group)

90–120 Days

Brussels sprouts have a central stem 2–3 feet high on which the 1- to 2-inch, cabbagelike heads form. Brussels sprouts are relatively hardy; they like cool weather and their flavor is improved by frost. They are usually grown as a winter crop in the South and a fall crop in the North.

GROWING TIPS

Start your own Brussels sprouts from seeds indoors or buy plants and set them into the garden 4 months before the first fall frost. Space them 18–24 inches apart in rows 30–36 inches apart. Brussels sprouts like rich, moist, well-drained soil. Fertilize prior to planting, when plants are 6–8 inches high, 12–15 inches high, and when the sprouts start to form. Mulch the plants and water them well. When the sprouts start to touch one another, remove lower leaves to provide more room. Harvest sprouts from the bottom up.

Cabbage *(Brassica oleracea,* Capitata Group) 70–80 Days

Cabbage forms globular heads of large, tightly wrapped, edible leaves. Green-leaved cabbage has smooth leaves; red cabbage has purplish-red leaves; and savoy cabbage has crinkled leaves. Cabbage is a fall through spring crop in the South and an early-summer or late-fall crop in the North. Early Jersey Wakefield is pictured.

GROWING TIPS

Purchase plants or start them from seeds and plant them as soon as the soil can be worked in spring. For a fall crop, you can sow seeds directly, ½ inch deep, or set out plants in midsummer to late summer. Space plants 15–18 inches apart in rows 24–30 inches apart. Cabbage grows best in moist, rich, well-drained soil. Fertilize at planting time and again once or twice with a quick-release fertilizer; mulch the soil to keep it cool. Harvest heads when they are well formed, firm, and glossy.

Chinese Cabbage
(Brassica rapa, Chinensis Group)

60 Days

Chinese cabbage, also called pak-choi, bok choy, or celery mustard, is an attractive leafy vegetable that gives good value for the space it occupies. The deep green leaves have a powdery bloom and broad, white stems. The inner leaves make a cluster but do not form a head.

GROWING TIPS

Chinese cabbage thrives in cool weather and does not like high summer heat. Direct-sow seeds, ½ inch deep, in early spring as soon as the soil can be worked or in late summer for a fall crop. Thin plants to stand 12–18 inches apart in rows 18–24 inches apart. Fertilize prior to planting and again in a month. Mulch the ground to keep it cool and moist. To harvest, cut off the entire plant at ground level or snap off the outer leaves.

Cape Gooseberry *(Physalis)*

Although cape gooseberries are also called ground husk tomatoes, they are not tomatoes. The fruits, which are up to 1 inch across, are formed within a loose, papery husk. Cape gooseberry, *P. peruviana,* is a sprawling vine; dwarf cape gooseberry, *P. pruinosa,* pictured, is smaller and more manageable. Tomatillos *(P. ixocarpa)* are larger, greener, and less sweet.

GROWING TIPS

Start cape gooseberry seeds indoors and transfer seedlings to the garden after all danger of frost has passed. Set plants 12 inches apart in sandy, well-drained soil. If they are planted in very rich soil or are fertilized too much they will bear few fruits. They like a warm growing season; use plastic mulch to keep the soil warm in cooler areas. When the fruits are ripe, the husks open and the fruits drop to the ground.

Carrot *(Daucus carota var. sativus)*

50–70 Days

Carrots usually have long, slender orange roots and bright green foliage, but there are now varieties in a wide range of sizes and shapes, with various growing needs. Royal Chantenay is pictured.

GROWING TIPS

Plant carrot seeds as soon as the soil can be worked in early spring and make successive sowings every 3 weeks for a continuous supply. Plant seeds ½ inch deep in most soils and ¼ inch deep in heavy soils.

Carrots germinate slowly. Thin plants so that they are 1–2 inches apart in rows 6 inches apart. Carrots will grow in any loose, moist, fertile soil that is free of stones, but do best in sandy soil. In heavy soils, plant a short variety because the very long ones won't thrive. Fertilize prior to planting and again when the greens are 6 inches tall. Mound soil over the tops of carrots to keep them from turning green. Harvest carrots when they are ¾–2 inches thick, depending on the variety.

Cauliflower
(*Brassica oleracea*, Botrytis Group)

50–70 Days

The edible part of cauliflower is the head of tightly clustered white or purple flower buds (the variety Purple Head is pictured). Cauliflowers grow best in cool weather and will withstand light frost.

GROWING TIPS
Set plants into the garden 2 weeks before the last spring frost or 3–3½ months before the first fall frost. It is important that the flower heads form during cool weather. Space plants 18 inches apart in rows 36 inches apart. Seeds can be directly sown, ½ inch deep. Cauliflower prefers rich, moist, well-drained soil. Fertilize prior to planting and again every 4 weeks during growth. Keep plants well watered and apply a mulch. The heads of most "white" varieties are naturally yellow; to make them white, pull the outer leaves over the heads when the heads are 2 inches across and tie the leaves with a string. To harvest, cut the stalk below the head while the buds are still tight.

Celeriac *(Apium graveolens* var. *rapaceum)* 90–120 Days

Celeriac, sometimes called knob celery or turnip-rooted celery, is grown for its knobby, globe-shaped root, which has a strong celery flavor. It is delicious julienned and dressed with a mild vinaigrette.

GROWING TIPS

Celeriac seeds are fine and slow to sprout. Start them indoors very early in winter and move plants to the garden in mid-spring to late spring, after nights are above 55° F. Space plants 6–12 inches apart. Soil must be very rich and constantly moist; a mulch will help. Remove any side shoots that develop. Celeriac's roots can be harvested at any time when they are 3–4 inches in diameter. They may be left in the ground all winter in mild areas.

Celery *(Apium graveolens* var. *dulce)*

Celery is a leafy, bushy, upright plant that reaches 30 inches high. It produces crisp, light green or yellow leafstalks that grow from 6–9 inches long. Celery needs 3–4 months of temperatures over 70° F but will not grow well where the weather is hot and dry.

GROWING TIPS

Purchase celery seedlings or grow your own indoors, starting them 10–12 weeks before moving them outside. It is best to wait until frost danger has passed to plant celery. Set plants in the garden 9–12 inches apart in rows 12 inches apart, in rich, constantly moist soil. Fertilize at planting time and monthly thereafter. Harvest the entire head or remove the outer stalks only.

Leaf Chicory *(Cichorium intybus)*

Chicory forms an 18-inch head of large, loose, dark green leaves, which are used in salads. Pain de Sucre Leaf Chicory is pictured. The roots of Magdeburg Chicory are ground and added to coffee. French or Belgian endive is also a type of chicory.

GROWING TIPS

Plant chicory seeds outdoors after danger of frost has passed, ½ inch deep and 4 inches apart in rows 18 inches apart. Thin plants to 12 inches apart as they grow. Average soil is adequate; fertilize prior to planting and again in 2 months. Pick leaves at any time until just before the first fall frost. The plants are quite hardy and if left in the ground will produce leaves for harvest every spring followed by light blue flowers in summer.

Collards *(Brassica oleracea,* Acephala Group) 80–90 Days

Collards do not form a true head but grow in a large rosette of blue-green leaves. Their flavor is improved by frost and they can withstand heat better than other members of the cabbage family. Even so, they are best grown as a cool-weather crop. To improve the flavor of leaves harvested in summer, place them in the refrigerator for a few days.

GROWING TIPS

Seeds or plants can go into the ground as soon as the soil can be worked in early spring or in mid-summer to late summer for a fall crop. Plant seeds ½ inch deep; space plants 15–18 inches apart in rows 18–24 inches apart. Collards grow best in rich, moist, well-drained soil. Fertilize prior to planting and again every 3–4 weeks. Mulch to keep the soil cool and moist. Harvest leaves as needed but do not disturb the plant's growing tip.

Sweet Corn (*Zea mays* var. *rugosa*)

Corn plants grow up to 9 feet tall and produce 1 or 2 ears each, with white, yellow, or bicolored kernels. Older varieties are sweetest when cooked within minutes of being picked, but new "supersweet" corn remains sweet up to 14 days after harvest.

GROWING TIPS

Corn is best grown from seed sown directly into the garden after all danger of frost has passed and the soil is warm. Plant seeds 2 inches deep and 4–6 inches apart in rows 2–3 feet apart. When the plants are a few inches high, thin them to 6–12 inches apart. Corn grows best in rich, well-drained soil. Corn must be planted in a block of at least 3 rows to ensure pollination. Supersweet corn must be grown by itself to prevent cross-pollination. Fertilize corn before planting and again when the plants are 18 inches high. Harvest when the silks start to turn brown and damp. Break ears off the plant with a downward twisting motion.

Cucumber *(Cucumis sativus)*

Cucumbers grow up to 10 inches long. Many cucumber vines have both male and female flowers; the female flowers form the fruits. There are also self-fertilizing varieties that form fruits without pollination; the fruits are seedless.

GROWING TIPS

Plant cucumber seeds or seedlings in the garden after all danger of frost has passed. Sow seeds 1 inch deep and 4–6 inches apart in rows 3 feet apart. Thin plants to 12 inches apart. Vining cucumbers can grow on a trellis or other support or they can be left to grow on the ground. Cucumbers grow best in rich, light, moist soil that is well drained and fertilized monthly. Slicing cucumbers are best harvested when they are about 7 inches long; cut them off with a knife. Harvest often to keep the plants productive.

Pickling Cucumber *(Cucumis sativus)*   50–75 Days

Cucumbers grown for pickling are usually shorter and blockier in shape than slicing cucumbers. Most cucumbers grow on sprawling vines that grow 6–8 feet high, but there are bushy varieties with short vines that can be grown in small gardens or containers. The variety Liberty is pictured.

GROWING TIPS
Grow pickling cucumbers in the same way as cucumbers for slicing. Harvest pickling cucumbers when they are 1½–3 inches long or leave them to grow larger for dill pickles.

Eggplant *(Solanum melongena var. esculentum)*   60–80 Days

Eggplants (sometimes called aubergine) bear egg-shaped, oval, or slender fruits that have smooth purple, black, or white skins and white meat. Black Beauty is pictured. Eggplants are warm-weather plants.

GROWING TIPS

Plant eggplant in the garden after all danger of frost has passed and the weather is evenly warm. Wait until nights are above 55° F; cool weather can deter growth. Eggplants can be directly sown only where the growing season is long; in other areas, purchase plants or start your own indoors. Set plants 2 feet apart in rows 2–3 feet apart. Fertilize prior to planting and again every 4–6 weeks; water deeply during dry weather. Black plastic mulch will keep the soil warm. Pick eggplants while their skin is still shiny.

Curly Endive *(Cichorium endiva)*

Curly endive has cut and curled leaves that grow in a 9-inch mound. Escarole, which is the same species, has smooth, broad leaves. Both resemble leaf lettuce and can be cooked or used fresh in salads; the inner leaves are best for salads and the outer leaves for cooking.

GROWING TIPS

Escarole and curly endive grow well only when the weather is cool. The leaves taste best if they are planted in midsummer to late summer in the North and in spring in the South. Start with seeds or plants and thin them to 12 inches apart. Mulch plants to keep the roots cool in warm areas. Fertilize at planting time and again about halfway through the growing season. To reduce bitterness, blanch the plants by covering them with bushel baskets for 2–3 weeks. Harvest the entire plant when it is mature.

Florence Fennel
(*Foeniculum vulgare* var. *azoricum*)

90–110 Days

Florence fennel, or finocchio, looks much like the herb fennel but has a swollen base comprised of tightly clasped, ribbed, solid stems. The finely divided apple-green foliage resembles dill but has the flavor and aroma of anise. Eat the bulbs raw or cooked and use the foliage as a garnish.

GROWING TIPS

Florence fennel develops best in cool weather. In the North, plant seedlings (they can be purchased or started indoors) in the garden 2–3 weeks before the last spring frost. Move them carefully; they dislike transplanting. Space the plants 6–12 inches apart. In the South, they can be set into the garden in late summer. To harvest, remove the entire plant from the ground and trim off the stems about an inch above the bulb.

Garlic (Allium sativum)

Garlic, a perennial commonly grown as an annual, is prized for its bulbs, which are made up of 7–10 segments called cloves that are encased in a papery white skin. If garlic is allowed to bloom, it produces round clusters of tiny white flowers.

GROWING TIPS

Garlic is grown from its cloves. Plant them in early spring to midspring for a late summer to fall harvest or in fall for a harvest the following spring or summer. Carefully break the cloves off from the main bulb and plant them so their tips are just below the soil surface. Space them 3–4 inches apart in rows 12 inches apart. Garlic grows best in light, sandy soil that is rich and well drained. Fertilize at planting time with a low-nitrogen fertilizer and feed again when the plants are 6 inches tall. When the foliage starts to turn yellow, bend it over without breaking it off to hasten ripening of the bulbs. Lift the bulbs when the leaves turn brown and dry them in the sun.

Ginger *(Zingiber officinale)*

Ginger is a frost-tender perennial that can be grown as an annual. It can become a pest in mild areas where soil is moist and fertile. In the North it is often grown in containers. The stems grow from a mat of edible, tuberous roots, which can be used fresh or dried to season stir-fry and other dishes.

GROWING TIPS

Plant pieces of ginger root in shallow, 5- to 10-gallon containers of potting soil or sand. In warm areas, you can move them to the garden when they have rooted, spacing the plants 12 inches apart. Grow ginger in light shade and water it often. In the North it benefits from reflected light and heat. In areas with freezing temperatures in winter, move containers indoors, allow the tops to dry off and turn yellow, then cut them back. Water only enough to keep the roots slightly moist. In spring, put the containers back outside. To harvest, dig the roots before fall frost and store them at room temperature.

Horseradish (*Armoracia rusticana*)

The thick white root of the horseradish plant is the source of the spicy, grated garnish of the same name. Horseradish is a perennial but it is usually grown as an annual because it is not as tasty after the first year. It can be grown in a deep container.

GROWING TIPS

To grow horseradish, plant root cuttings in spring or fall, 2–3 inches deep and 12 inches apart. Horseradish prefers rich soil; it will not do well in sandy soil. Fertilize at planting time; no further feeding is necessary. Harvest roots in the fall and winter as needed. Pieces of root that remain in the soil will grow into new plants the following year; harvest horseradish every year to keep it from invading the garden.

Jerusalem Artichoke
(Helianthus tuberosus)

120–150 Days

Jerusalem artichoke, neither an artichoke nor from Jerusalem, is a close relative of the sunflower. It can grow 6–12 feet high and has large, daisylike yellow flowers but is grown for its edible, potato-like tubers, which have a sweet flavor and can be eaten raw or cooked.

GROWING TIPS

Grow Jerusalem artichokes from small tubers; if you divide larger tubers, be sure each division has at least 1 eye. Plant the tubers in spring or fall, 2 inches deep and 15–24 inches apart in rows 30 inches apart. Average, well-drained soil is sufficient; soil too rich leads to invasive growth. Water the plants when the soil is dry. Remove flowers as they form to induce larger tubers. Jerusalem artichoke should be grown in a bed by itself, as it tends to take over an area. Any small piece of root left in the ground will produce a new plant. Dig the tubers planted in spring when the leaves die back in fall; dry them and store in a cool, dry place.

Kale *(Brassica oleracea,* Acephala Group*)*

Kale grows in open rosettes of blue-green, finely cut or curled leaves. Although it is a hardy perennial, it is usually grown as an annual because the leaves become tough and stringy in older plants. It is slightly resistant to heat and can be grown during the summer but is better as a late-spring or fall crop.

GROWING TIPS
Plant kale in early spring as soon as the soil can be worked or in mid-summer to late summer. Sow seeds directly, ¼ inch deep, or start with plants, setting them 12–15 inches apart in rows 18–24 inches apart. Kale grows best in rich, moist, well-drained soil. Fertilize prior to planting and again every month; mulch to keep the soil cool and moist. To harvest kale, cut the entire plant or take the larger leaves, leaving the younger ones to grow. Frost improves the flavor of kale; place leaves harvested before frost in the refrigerator for several days before cooking them.

Kohlrabi
(*Brassica oleracea*, Gongylodes Group)

50–60 Days

Kohlrabi is grown for the swollen lower portion of the stem, which forms just above ground level. These "bulbs" are greenish white or purple. Leaves sprout from all over the vegetable, giving it a most unusual appearance. Kohlrabi prefers cool weather but can be grown as a summer crop in all areas but the deep South.

GROWING TIPS

Move kohlrabi plants into the garden as soon as the soil can be worked in early spring, or in late summer. Seeds can be directly sown, ¼ inch deep, in rows 15–18 inches apart. Final spacing for plants should be 6 inches apart. Kohlrabi will grow in light shade. It grows best in deep, rich soil that is moist and well drained; apply a mulch to keep it cool. Fertilize prior to planting and again every month. Harvest kohlrabi when it is young and tender and the bulb is 2–2½ inches across.

Leek *(Allium ampeloprasum, Porrum Group)*   80–110 Days

Leeks are related to onions and have a mild, delicate, sweet flavor. They do not form bulbs but produce a thick, cylindrical stalk up to 18 inches long. The foliage, also edible, grows in an arching habit.

GROWING TIPS

Purchase leek seedlings or start seeds indoors 6–10 weeks before moving seedlings outside in early spring to mid-spring, when they are about ¼ inch thick. Space them 3–6 inches apart in rows 12 inches apart. They grow best in rich soil that is kept evenly moist at all times. Fertilize at planting time with a low-nitrogen fertilizer and again when plants are 6–9 inches tall. As they grow, mound soil around the base of the stem to keep it white. Harvest leeks in the fall when the stems are at least ¾ inch thick; they are sweetest when they are about 1½ inches thick. They can be left in the ground all winter and harvested the following spring if the temperature stays above 10° F.

Butterhead Lettuce *(Lactuca sativa)* 62–75 Days

Butterhead lettuce has crisp, fleshy, delicate leaves of light to dark green that grow into a small, loose, open, but distinct, head. The interior of the head is creamy white. Bibb Butterhead is pictured.

GROWING TIPS

Grow butterhead lettuce from plants—either purchase them or start your own indoors—or from seeds. Place seeds or plants in the garden as soon as the soil can be worked in spring. Sow the seeds 3 inches apart; do not cover them. Thin plants to 10 inches apart. They will grow best in moist, well-drained, fertile soil, which forces fast growth. Butterhead lettuce bolts to seed when weather becomes hot, but a second crop can be sown in late summer through fall. Buttercrunch is a heat-resistant variety. To harvest, pick outer leaves or cut the entire head when it matures.

Crisphead Lettuce *(Lactuca sativa)*

Crisphead lettuce, also called iceberg lettuce, has a tight, firm head of crisp, brittle leaves. Although it is the lettuce most commonly found in the supermarket, it is the most difficult to grow in the home garden because it is slow to mature and does not grow well in the heat. Great Lakes Crisphead is pictured.

GROWING TIPS

Crisphead varieties are best started from purchased seedlings or from plants started indoors in late winter. Plant them in the garden as soon as the soil can be worked in spring, spacing plants 12 inches apart. Plants can be added to the garden every 2 weeks for a continuous harvest if summer temperatures do not rise above 75° F. Elsewhere it can be grown more successfully in fall. All types of lettuce grow best in fertile soil that is moist and well drained. Harvest crisphead lettuce when the center of the head is firm.

Leaf Lettuce *(Lactuca sativa)*

Leaf lettuce has frilled, curled, crinkled, or oaklike leaves of light to dark green or reddish bronze that do not form heads. It matures quickly and is the easiest lettuce to grow in the home garden. Red Salad Bowl is the variety shown here.

GROWING TIPS

Leaf lettuce is usually grown from seeds because it matures so quickly, although it can also be grown from plants. Place plants or seeds in the garden as soon as the soil can be worked in spring; sow a second crop after the hottest days of summer are over. Sow the seeds 3 inches apart, uncovered, and thin the seedlings to 6 inches apart. Leaf lettuce is one of the more heat-resistant lettuces. All types of lettuce, but leaf lettuce especially, taste best if they grow rapidly, so fertilize the plants every 3 weeks. Harvest leaf lettuce by picking the outer leaves when they are large enough.

Romaine Lettuce *(Lactuca sativa)*

Romaine, or cos, lettuce has an upright, cylindrical head with firmly wrapped leaves that are light to medium green. The interior of the head is cream colored. Romaine lettuce is slightly sweeter than leaf and butterhead and takes longer to grow. Paris White Cos is the variety pictured here.

GROWING TIPS

If you plant romaine lettuce in spring, use purchased plants or plants started indoors in late winter. Place the plants in the garden 2–3 weeks before the last frost. For better results, sow seeds directly in late summer or fall. Space the seeds 3 inches apart, leaving them uncovered, and thin the plants to 10 inches apart. Pick the outer leaves as needed or cut the entire head off at ground level when it is mature.

Honeydew Melon
(*Cucumis melo*, Inodorus Group)

80–90 Days

The melons in this group, which also includes casaba and crenshaw melons, are known collectively as winter melons. The vines are large and sprawling; the fruits have smooth or lightly ridged white, yellow, or yellowish-green skin and light green or white flesh. The winter melons are a long-season, late-maturing fruit.

GROWING TIPS

Sow melon seeds 2 weeks after the last spring frost, setting them ½ inch deep in rows 4 feet apart. In areas with short, cool growing seasons, start seeds indoors 5–6 weeks earlier. Thin plants to 12 inches apart. Where summers are short, use clear plastic mulch to trap heat and encourage dense growth. All melons must have excellent drainage to grow well; plant them in raised beds to improve drainage. Fertilize before planting and every 4 weeks. Water during the growing season but decrease watering when the fruit is ripening; too much water will destroy the flavor. Harvest when the melon comes cleanly off the stem with a little pressure.

Muskmelon
(Cucumis melo, Reticulatus Group)

65–90 Days

Although we often call this melon cantaloupe, the true cantaloupe is rarely grown in this country. Muskmelons grow on large, vining plants that reach up to 10 feet across. The fruit is ribbed and has netting on the skin; the flesh is orange. Sweet 'n' Early is pictured.

GROWING TIPS

Muskmelons are grown and harvested in the same way as honeydew melons. Use black plastic mulch to warm up the soil and aid growth in areas with short growing seasons. Muskmelons are ready to harvest when the stem slips easily from the melon with slight pressure.

Watermelon *(Citrullus lanatus)* 75–95 Days

Watermelons grow on large, sprawling vines. The fruit is round, oval, or oblong with smooth skin that varies from light to dark green and is often striped. The flesh is usually red but can be yellow or white. There are space-saving watermelons with more compact growth. Sugar Baby is seen here.

Growing Tips

Watermelon needs a long growing season; in areas with short summers, start from plants or choose an early-ripening variety. Black or clear plastic mulch will warm up the soil and assist growth. Watermelons grow best in sandy soil. Place seeds or plants in the garden 2 weeks after all danger of frost has passed in spring. Space plants 3 feet apart in rows 4 feet apart. Keep the plants well watered during their growing season but allow them to dry out when they are ripening. You know that a watermelon is ripe if it makes a dull sound if rapped, if the spot where it lies on the ground turns golden-yellow, or if the tendrils where the fruit joins the vine turn brown.

Mustard Greens (*Brassica juncea*)

40–50 Day

Mustard greens is a spinach-like plant that grows 12 inches high. The cut, crisped, frilled, or curled leaves are yellowish to medium green and have a slightly peppery flavor.

Growing Tips

Mustard greens have a short growing period. Sow seeds ¼ inch deep, 1–2 inches apart in rows 12 inches apart, beginning in early spring. Thin plants to 12 inches apart. Stop sowing in early summer—mustard greens do not like heat—and resume sowing 6–8 weeks before the first fall frost. In the South, mustard greens can be grown throughout most of the winter. They grow best in rich, moist soil that is well drained. Fertilize at planting time and again in 3 weeks. Mulch to keep the soil cool and moist. Harvest the outside leaves when they are 3–inches long and still tender, leaving the inner leaves to develop.

Okra *(Abelmoschus esculentus)*

55–70 Days

Okra, the main ingredient in gumbo and other Creole dishes, grows 3–8 feet tall. It bears large, funnel-shaped flowers that are pale yellow with a maroon center. They are followed by the long, slender, pointed and ribbed pods. Clemson Spineless Okra is pictured.

Growing Tips

Okra is a warm-weather vegetable and should not be planted in the garden until 2 weeks after the last spring frost. Sow seeds ½–¾ inch deep in rows spaced 3 feet apart and thin seedlings to 18–24 inches apart. Where summers are short, start with plants or start seeds indoors in mid-spring. Soak seeds in water for 24 hours before sowing them. Okra grows best in heavy, moderately fertile soil that is well drained. Fertilize prior to planting, again when plants are 12 inches tall, and when they flower. Pick okra pods when they are young and tender and about 3–5 inches long.

Long-Day Onion
(*Allium cepa*, Cepa Group)

75–100 Days

Onions are classified as long-day or short-day. The long-day varieties form bulbs only during long days and are usually grown in the North in summer. Yellow Spanish Onion is pictured.

GROWING TIPS

Long-day onions are grown from seeds, transplants, or sets (dried bulbs). Seeds are best started indoors. Move sets or seedlings to the garden in mid-spring and plant them in rows 12 inches apart. Plant sets 1 inch deep. Space the plants a little farther apart than their mature diameter. They grow best in rich, well-worked soil. Fertilize at planting time and again twice during the growing season. When the tops start to turn brown, bend them over without breaking them to hasten ripening of the onions. Several days later, lift the onions from the soil with a spading fork and dry them in the sun for a week until their necks are dry.

Short-Day Onion
(*Allium cepa*, Cepa Group)

Short-day onions form bulbs only during short days and are usually grown in the South in winter and spring. Italian Red Onion is the variety shown.

Growing Tips

Short-day onions are grown from seeds or transplants. Seeds can be started indoors or can be directly sown, ¼–½ inch deep, in areas with long growing seasons. Move seedlings to the garden in late summer or fall and plant them in rows 12 inches apart. The spacing should be slightly greater than their mature diameter. Onions grow best in fertile soil with all lumps and stones removed. Fertilize at planting time and again twice during the growing season. Short-day onions are harvested in the same way as long-day onions. Select onion varieties carefully; some store much better than others.

Root Parsley
(Petroselinum crispum var. *tuberosum)* 80–95 Days

Root parsley, also called turnip parsley, is related to the herb parsley and resembles the flat-leaved varieties. The edible roots are creamy white and slender and taste something like celeriac.

GROWING TIPS
Root parsley is grown from seeds, but they are slow to germinate. Soak them in water for 24 hours before sowing to speed up germination. Sow 2–4 weeks before the last spring frost, ¼ inch deep, in rows 12 inches apart. Thin plants to 6–8 inches apart. They grow best in deeply prepared soil that is rich, moist, and sandy. Fertilize at planting time and again in 1 month. In late fall, loosen the soil and pull the roots as you need them. Cold intensifies their flavor and sweetness. In areas with mild winters roots can remain in the ground all winter but must be harvested before the plants grow and flower in spring.

Parsnip <i>(Pastinaca sativa)</i>

120–150 Days

Parsnips have large, white, carrotlike roots that have a sweet flavor. Seeds are sown in spring for fall harvest in the North and in late summer for winter harvest in the South.

GROWING TIPS

Parsnips are grown from seeds, which are short-lived, slow to germinate, and have a low germination rate. Sow them thickly and cover them with leaf mold, sand, or peat moss. The germination rate may be improved by soaking the seeds in warm water for 24 hours before sowing them. Sow seeds ½ inch deep and 1 inch apart in rows 15–18 inches apart. They prefer deeply prepared, fertile, loose soil that is free of stones and debris. Fertilize prior to planting and again midway through the growing season. Weed often and water the plants well. Dig the roots after frost, which improves their flavor; store them in the refrigerator to sweeten them.

Edible-Podded Pea
(*Pisum sativum* var. *macrocarpon*)

60–70 Days

The edible-podded peas include snow peas (pictured here) and sugar snap peas. They have the tenderness and fleshy qualities of snap beans and the flavor and sweetness of fresh green peas. When young, the peas are not shelled but are cooked pod and all. At this stage, the pods are stringless, brittle, and free of fiber.

GROWING TIPS

Edible-podded peas are grown in the same way as green peas. Pick snow peas when they are young, succulent, and still flat, about 1½–3 inches long. Harvest sugar snap peas, which have more rounded pods, anytime until the pods turn yellow. Their flavor is at its best when they are full sized and have begun to develop a pebbly surface and to fade in color.

Green Pea (*Pisum sativum*)

Green peas, or English peas, which are a cool-weather crop, grow on shrubby or vining plants. They are best grown in spring and fall in the North and in fall, winter, and spring in the South. Remove green peas from the pods before cooking them. The variety Burpee Blue Bantam is pictured here.

Growing Tips

Spring plantings give the largest yields in most areas, so plant peas very early, as soon as the soil can be worked. Treat the soil or the seeds with a bacterial inoculant to help the plants extract nitrogen from the air. Plant seeds 1–2 inches deep; set the shrubby varieties in rows 18–24 inches apart and the vining types in rows 30–36 inches apart. Thin plants to 1–2 inches apart. Vining types need a trellis or other support. Peas are particular about soil; they grow best in deep, fertile, sandy soil that is well drained. They need no fertilizing. Pick peas when the pods are fully swollen and round and before the seeds become hard.

Peanut *(Arachis hypogaea)*

Peanuts are neat, attractive plants; some are bushy, others trailing. The yellow female flowers are pealike; when pollinated, they turn face down and corkscrew into the ground. Each corkscrew, or peg, develops 1–4 peanuts, 2–6 inches below the soil surface. Peanuts need a long, hot growing season.

GROWING TIPS

Peanuts grow best in sandy, fertile soil that is well worked and high in organic matter. Plant seeds 1 inch deep and 12 inches apart in rows 2–2½ feet apart after all danger of frost has passed in spring. It is not necessary to shell the seeds but it will hasten germination. Space the plants 2–3 feet apart. Water well during the growing season but stop watering when the peanuts start to ripen. Dig up the plant with a spading fork when the leaves start to turn yellow and before the first fall frost and remove the peanuts.

Hot Pepper *(Capsicum annuum)*

Hot peppers, which are usually long and thin, cone shaped, or small and round, grow on 20- to 30-inch-tall plants. All belong to the same species as sweet peppers except for tabasco *(C. frutescens)*. The medium-hot variety Anaheim is pictured.

Growing Tips

Move hot pepper plants (buy them or start them indoors 8–12 weeks earlier) into the garden after all danger of frost has passed and the soil is warm. Seeds can be sown outdoors only where summers are very long. Space plants 18–24 inches apart in rows 30 inches apart. They prefer rich, well-drained soil. Fertilize at planting time and again in 6 weeks; too much fertilizer will cause lush growth but few fruits. Hot peppers mature somewhat later than sweet peppers and need more heat to produce. Black plastic mulch will help to keep the ground warm. Harvest when the peppers turn red. Hot peppers can irritate the skin; wear gloves when handling them.

Sweet Pepper (*Capsicum annuum*)

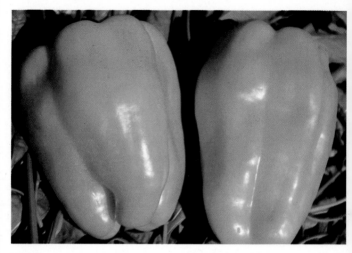

Most sweet peppers are bell shaped or wedge shaped, but there are also varieties that are tapered or round. Sweet peppers are green, purple, or yellow, and most of them will turn red if allowed to ripen fully on the plant. The variety Golden California Wonder is pictured here.

GROWING TIPS

Sweet peppers are grown in the same way as hot peppers. Peppers will produce only a certain number of fruits at one time; when that number is reached, they stop producing. After those fruits are harvested, the plants will start to produce again. Sweet peppers are usually harvested when firm and green.

Baking Potato *(Solanum tuberosum)*

90–120 Days

Baking potatoes have dry, mealy flesh and thick, whitish skin and are the best potatoes for storing. Most, but not all, baking potatoes form oblong tubers. Katahdin is the variety pictured.

GROWING TIPS

Potatoes are grown from pieces of mature tubers known as "seed potatoes." Purchased seed potatoes are best because they are certified to be free of disease. Make sure each has at least 1 eye. Plant them in early spring about 6 weeks before the last frost, setting them 4–5 inches deep and 12–15 inches apart. They grow best in sandy, rich, acid soil that is well drained. Add fertilizer before planting; no further feeding is needed. Mound soil around the tubers to keep out light, which turns potatoes green and bitter. When the tops of the plants die back, loosen the soil and gently lift the potatoes from the ground.

Boiling Potato *(Solanum tuberosum)*

Boiling potatoes have moist white flesh and thin white or red skin. They can be used for frying as well as boiling. Red LaSoda is pictured.

GROWING TIPS

Although a few varieties of potatoes can be grown from seeds, they are usually grown from seed potatoes. See Baking Potato for specific planting information. Plant potatoes as early in spring as weather permits; it may help to prepare the soil the previous fall. Do not plant when the soil is still cold and wet; it may cause the seed potato to rot. When plants are 6 inches tall, mound soil over the roots to keep the potatoes from turning green; repeat when the plants are 18 inches high. For "new" potatoes, dig some of the tubers when the plants are flowering. Leave some potatoes to harvest in the fall.

Sweet Potato (*Ipomoea batatas*)

Sweet potatoes, often incorrectly called yams, have oblong, edible roots with flesh that ranges from pale yellow to orange. The plants are low-growing vines with dark green, pointed leaves and funnel-shaped flowers.

GROWING TIPS

Sweet potatoes are grown from slips, which are rooted cuttings grown from seed potatoes (pieces of potato with at least 1 growing eye). Plant slips outdoors after all danger of frost has passed and the soil is warm. Space them 15–18 inches apart; plant the bottom of the slip 5–6 inches below soil level. Sweet potatoes grow best in dry soil that is sandy and well drained. Fertilize prior to planting but not again. Sweet potatoes are heat tolerant and drought resistant. In the North, grow short-season cultivars. Harvest sweet potatoes just before the first fall frost.

Pumpkin (*Cucurbita*)

Pumpkins, which are related to winter squashes, are of 2 species. *C. pepo* includes the small pumpkins that grow to 20 pounds and are popular for carving and cooking. *C. maxima* are the large pumpkins that grow from 20–100 pounds (Big Max Mammoth is pictured). Both species grow on sprawling, 10-foot vines or bushy, 3-foot plants.

GROWING TIPS

Sow pumpkin seeds in the garden after danger of frost has passed, setting them ½–1 inch deep. You can purchase plants or start them indoors but they do not transplant well. Space vining plants 4 feet apart and bush varieties 3 feet apart in rows 6–10 feet apart, depending on plant habit. Pumpkins tolerate light shade and they like rich, well-drained soil. Fertilize at planting time and again every month. Harvest in fall before hard frost when the vines start to die. Prop fruits off the ground to prevent rotting.

Radicchio *(Cichorium intybus)*

Radicchio is a type of leaf chicory. It resembles a small red cabbage and is used in salads. It forms a tight head of deep red or magenta leaves veined in white. Rouge di Verona is shown here.

GROWING TIPS

Plant radicchio seeds outdoors, 8–10 inches apart, in mid-spring in the North and in late summer in the South. Radicchio needs a long, cool season to develop. It grows well in average, well-drained soil; keep the soil cool and moist with a mulch in hot areas. Older varieties of radicchio take about 8 months to mature. They send up very long, hairy, dark green leaves early in their growing cycle, which must be cut back to force the head of red leaves to develop. There are new, fast-growing varieties that mature in about half the time and need no cutting back. Many seed companies now offer these; 'Marina' is one variety. Radicchio planted in spring is harvested in fall; that planted in late summer is harvested in late winter or early spring.

Spring Radish *(Raphanus sativus)*

Radishes have enlarged, edible roots that are round, oval, cylindrical, or tapered like an icicle. They may be white, red, pink, or purple, or a combination of these colors. Champion is the variety pictured here.

GROWING TIPS

Spring radishes tolerate cold but not heat; they can be grown successfully in spring or fall. They taste best when grown quickly in fertile soil. Sow seeds in early spring as soon as the soil can be worked, ⅛–¼ inch deep and 1 inch apart. Sow successively every 2 weeks until midspring and sow again in early fall. Thin seedlings to 1–2 inches apart. They grow best in sandy soil; if your soil is heavy, grow radishes in raised beds. Fertilize at planting time and again every 2 weeks. Radishes are ready to harvest about 3–4 weeks after germination, when they are about ¾ inch wide and still crisp. The leaves can be cooked with other greens.

Winter Radish
(Raphanus sativus var. longipinnatus)

60–80 Days

Growing Tips

Also called daikon or Oriental radish, winter radish is more pungent than spring radish and has larger roots, which are rounded or cylindrical.

Growing Tips

Plant winter radish seeds in late summer or early fall. If you plant them too soon, the plants may bolt to seed before they can form worthwhile roots. Sow seeds ½ inch deep and an inch apart in rows 6–12 inches apart. As the plants grow, thin them to 6–12 inches apart. They prefer rich, moist soil that is loose and sandy. Fertilize at planting time and again every 2 weeks to encourage quick growth. In northern areas, apply a mulch of straw or pine needles. Harvest winter radishes about 2–2½ months after planting; they are not damaged by fall frost. The young greens are also edible.

Rhubarb (*Rheum rhabarbarum*)

Rhubarb has tart, fleshy, pink to red leafstalks that are used to make desserts. The stalks grow 1–2½ feet long from the base of the plant and bear large, reddish-green leaves. Although the stalks are edible, the leaves are poisonous and should never be eaten.

GROWING TIPS

Rhubarb, hardy to zone 4, grows best where summers are warm and moist and winters are cold enough to freeze the ground. In hot areas, plant them in afternoon shade. Rhubarb can be grown from seeds, but divisions produce better plants. Set plants 3–4 feet apart in rich, deeply prepared, well-drained soil. Fertilize every year in spring when growth starts. Divide every few years if necessary. Do not harvest until plants are in their second or third year. From spring to early summer, snap off up to half of the outer leafstalks; use only the stalks, never the leaves.

Rutabaga

(*Brassica napus,* Napobrassica Group)

90–120 Days

Rutabaga, sometimes called Swedish turnip, is closely related to the turnip. It is a cool-season vegetable grown in fall through spring in the South and in fall in the North. Rutabagas have large, fine, globe-shaped roots with either white or yellow flesh; the white is better for eating fresh.

GROWING TIPS

Rutabaga should be planted as late as possible so it will mature just before the ground freezes. This is generally about 3–3½ months before the first fall frost. Sow seeds ½ inch deep and 3–4 inches apart in rows 18–24 inches apart. Thin plants to 6–8 inches apart. They prefer rich, loose soil that is moist and well drained. Harvest rutabagas when they are at least 3–4 inches wide. As long as the ground is not frozen, you can leave them there until you are ready to use them.

Salsify *(Tragopogon porrifolius)*

Salsify is sometimes called vegetable oyster because its flavor is reminiscent of oysters. The plants have large clumps of broad, grass-like leaves and a heavy, deep, edible taproot that can grow to 2½ inches wide and 16 inches long.

GROWING TIPS

Sow salsify seeds ¼ inch deep and 2 inches apart in rows 3 feet apart, 2–3 weeks before the last spring frost. Thin the plants to 4–6 inches apart. They prefer loose, deeply prepared soil that is sandy and well drained. Incorporate fertilizer at planting time and feed again monthly. Water when the ground is dry to prevent the roots from splitting. Salsify may be left in the ground over winter or harvested in late fall.

Scallion
(Allium fistulosum)

Scallions may be immature bulbous onions *(A. cepa),* or they may be bunching onions, *A. fistulosum* (pictured), which develop only very small bulbs or no bulbs at all. Bunching onions send up tubular green stems from the base of the plant; they continue to divide and sprout new stems throughout the growing season.

Growing Tips

To grow bunching onions or bulbous onions for scallions, plant seeds or small purchased bulbs in early spring, spacing them 2–3 inches apart. They grow best in rich soil that is loose and well drained. Fertilize at planting time and twice more during the season. Harvest them as soon as the stems are large enough. When harvesting bunching onions, remove only half of the stems; in 4–6 weeks, they may be harvested again. Scallions become more pungent the longer they remain in the ground.

Shallot (*Allium cepa*, Aggregatum Group) 90–120 Days

Shallots, often used as a substitute for onions in recipes, have a more delicate and subtle flavor. The bulbs have 3 or 4 segments called cloves. The leaves are long and tubular like scallions and are edible.

GROWING TIPS

Grow shallots from cloves, inserting each clove into the soil so the tip is just below the surface. Space the cloves 3–6 inches apart in rows 6 inches apart. Plant them in early spring as soon as the soil can be worked. In the hot South and West, plant them in fall for spring harvest. They prefer loose, rich soil with good drainage. Apply a low-nitrogen fertilizer at planting time and again halfway through the growing season. Harvest young shallots at any time and use them like scallions. Harvest mature bulbs in fall when the foliage starts to turn brown. To speed ripening, bend the foliage over without breaking it off; dig the bulbs up in 5 days.

Spinach *(Spinacia oleracea)*

Spinach is a cool-weather plant that is grown in spring and fall in most areas; it can be grown in winter in the South. Its long-stemmed leaves grow in a mound 12 inches high and 18 inches wide. Melody is the variety pictured.

GROWING TIPS
Spinach prefers moist, fertile, well-drained soil. It will not grow well in acid soil, so add lime if necessary to raise pH. Sow spinach seeds start-ing in early spring as soon as the soil can be worked; sow again in late summer up to 6 weeks before nights are 20° F. To hasten germination, store seeds in the refrigerator for 1 week before sowing. Sow seeds ½ inch deep and 2 inches apart in rows 15–18 inches apart. Thin plants to 4–5 inches apart. When the leaves are 6–8 inches long and before the plant flowers, cut off the outer leaves or cut the entire plant off at ground level to harvest it.

New Zealand Spinach
(Tetragonia tetragonioides)

60–90 Days

New Zealand spinach is grown as a substitute where it is too hot to grow spinach. It is a large plant with thick, succulent leaves and stems and a branching and spreading habit. It thrives in hot weather.

Growing Tips

Sow New Zealand spinach seeds directly in the garden; soak the seeds in hot water for several hours before sowing them. Plant the seeds 1–1½ inches deep and 8–10 inches apart in rows 3 feet apart after all danger of frost has passed. Thin plants to 1½ feet apart. They prefer soil that is rich and well drained; they will tolerate dry soil but grow better with regular watering. Light afternoon shade will keep the plants from wilting in hot weather. Harvest the young leaves at the tips of the plants at any time.

Acorn Squash *(Cucurbita pepo)*

Acorn squash and the closely related spaghetti squash are
known as winter squashes because
they store well during the winter.
Acorn squash is deeply ribbed and
shaped like an acorn, with dark
green, sometimes orange-streaked
skin. Spaghetti squash is oval and
has smooth, light yellow skin; its
flesh separates into strings when it
is cooked.

GROWING TIPS

All winter squashes can be started
from seeds or from seedlings (buy
seedlings or start seeds indoors in
mid-spring). Seedlings do not transplant well and are best started in
individual pots. Plant seeds or seedlings in the garden in the late spring
after all danger of frost has passed.
Plant seeds ½ inch deep in rows 6
feet apart; space the plants 4 feet
apart. Harvest acorn and spaghetti
squash before hard frost, when the
rind becomes hard.

Butternut Squash *(Cucurbita moschata)* 75–85 Days

Butternut squash is one of the winter squashes—it is harvested in mid-fall to late fall and can be stored through the winter. Butternut squash has a round, bulbous base and a narrow neck. Like all winter squashes, it grows on a vine that is 8–12 inches high and several feet long.

GROWING TIPS

Butternut squash is grown in the same way as acorn squash. All types of squash prefer rich and well-drained soil. Fertilize prior to planting and again once a month during the growing season. When harvesting squash, leave a piece of the stem on the fruit—the scar left when a squash is separated from its stem can begin to rot in storage.

Crookneck Squash *(Cucurbita pepo)*

A summer squash, crookneck squash has a tapering body and a curved neck. The skin is yellow and the flesh is yellow to off-white; some varieties have warty skin and others are smooth-skinned. Harvest and eat summer squash during the summer before the skin becomes hard.

GROWING TIPS

Summer squashes are tender; set seeds or plants into the garden after all danger of frost has passed. Sow seeds ½ inch deep and 18 inches apart in rows 5 feet apart. Thin seedlings to 3 feet apart. You can start seeds indoors in mid-spring; grow them in individual pots so the roots are not disturbed during transplanting. Summer squash prefers rich, well-drained soil. Harvest crookneck squash when it is about 5 inches long and 1½–2 inches wide.

Hubbard Squash *(Cucurbita maxima)* 90–120 Days

Hubbard squash and turban squash, which are the same species, are winter squashes. They have thick skins and store well over the winter. Hubbard squashes are rounded to tapered vegetables with ribbed, bumpy skin that is dark green, blue-green, whitish, or gold. The turban squashes are round and flattened and have a thick, round center that looks like a turban. They are often striped in bright red, orange, or white.

GROWING TIPS

Cultivate hubbard and turban squash in the same way as acorn and butternut squash. They are vining plants whose fruit is mature and ready for harvest just before hard fall frosts. Store winter squashes in a dry place.

Scallop Squash *(Cucurbita pepo)*

50–55 Days

Scallop squash, also called patty pan, is bowl shaped with scalloped edges. The skin of the fruit is light or dark green or yellow; the flesh is creamy white to pale yellow. Scallop squash is considered a summer squash.

GROWING TIPS

Follow the directions given for crookneck squash. Scallop squash likes fertile, well-drained soil; incorporate fertilizer into the soil prior to planting, and feed again every 3–4 weeks. All summer squashes are resistant to heat, but be sure to water them when the soil starts to dry out. In cooler areas, use black plastic mulch to keep the ground warm and aid in fruit production as well as weed control. The fruit is most tender and flavorful when it is 3–4 inches in diameter.

Straightneck Squash *(Cucurbita pepo)* 50–55 Days

Straightneck squash, a summer squash, has long, smooth, tapered fruits that do not have a distinct neck. They are harvested when they are still immature and the creamy or bright yellow skin is still soft. Early Prolific is pictured here.

Growing Tips
Straightneck squash is grown in the same manner as the other summer squashes; see Crookneck and Scallop squash for specific planting infor-

mation. Straightneck squash can be left on the plant to grow but is best if harvested when it is 5 inches long and 1½–2 inches thick. Pick fruit when the skin is still soft and can be pricked easily with your fingernail. Squash grows quickly, so check plants every day to see if there is any fruit ready for harvest. Plants that are harvested frequently will keep producing. You can damage the plant by pulling squash off, so cut them off with a knife or shears.

Zucchini Squash *(Cucurbita pepo)*

50–55 Days

Zucchini squash has straight, cylindrical fruits with yellow, gray, green, or black skin. Its large, yellow, trumpet-shaped flowers are also edible (don't eat all of them or you will have no fruits).

GROWING TIPS

Zucchini is a summer squash; see Crookneck, Scallop, and Straightneck squash for additional growing information. Pick zucchini when it is about 5 inches long and 2 inches across. Hard-skinned, mature fruits will store for a few weeks but are not as tasty and are better if peeled. The leaves of summer squash often develop a white, mottled appearance that resembles mildew disease but is harmless.

Strawberry *(Fragaria × ananassa)*

Strawberries are perennial plants that have 3 toothed leaflets per leaf and small white flowers. Some varieties produce one crop in early summer; others bear fruit all summer. The plants send out long runners; new plantlets form and easily root at the ends of the runners.

Growing Tips

Plant strawberry plants in early spring in the North and in fall in the South. They grow best in rich, light soil that is sandy and well drained. If your soil is heavy, grow strawberries in raised beds. Set the plants 2 feet apart in rows 6 feet apart or grow them in special tiered planters. Fertilize in early spring when growth starts and again in late summer. Mulch to increase fruit production and retain moisture. When plantings become crowded, remove the original plants and allow the plantlets to grow, transplanting them if necessary. Pick berries as soon as they are red and ripe. Strawberries planted in spring in the North will bear fruit the following year; those planted in fall in the South will fruit the next spring.

Sunflower *(Helianthus annuus)*

Depending on the variety, sunflowers grow from 1–12 feet tall. They are coarse plants with sticky, hairy leaves and large, golden-yellow, daisylike flowers. Some flowers have a contrasting center. Sunflower seeds are edible and nutritious.

GROWING TIPS

Sow sunflower seeds outdoors 1–2 weeks before the last spring frost. Mature plants are frost tender, but seeds and young seedlings tolerate cool weather. Space plants 1–4 feet apart, depending on their ultimate height. They grow best in light, dry, well-drained soil and need no fertilizing. In windy locations, stake sunflowers or tie them to fences. When seeds start to form, wrap cheesecloth around the flower heads to prevent birds from pilfering them. Test the seeds with your fingernail; when they are hard, cut the flower stems 6 inches below the heads and hang them indoors to dry.

Swiss Chard (*Beta vulgaris,* Cicla Group)   55–65 Days

Swiss chard is a relative of the beet that is grown for its greens instead of its root. It grows 18–24 inches high and has coarse, red or green leaves with a thick central rib that is red or white.

Growing Tips

Sow Swiss chard seeds outdoors 2–3 weeks before the last spring frost. In mild areas, sow seeds in late summer for a fall crop. Plant seeds 1 inch deep and 3 inches apart in rows 15–18 inches apart. Thin plants to stand 6 inches apart and use the thinnings as soup greens. Swiss chard will tolerate light shade but grows better in full sun. It thrives in loose, rich, well-drained soil that has a neutral pH. For best results, water often and fertilize prior to planting and again in 6 weeks. Cut off the outer leaves at the base of the plant when they reach full size. Inner leaves will continue to grow for later harvesting.

Cherry Tomato
(Lycopersicon lycopersicum var. *cerasiforme)*

60–70 Days

The small size of cherry tomatoes (¾–1 inch) has no relation to the size of the plant. Some grow on dwarf plants, but others grow on full-sized vines. Depending on the variety, cherry tomatoes may be determinate or indeterminate. Determinate cherry tomatoes grow well in containers or hanging baskets.

GROWING TIPS

Grow cherry tomatoes in the same way as other tomatoes; see Determinate and Indeterminate tomatoes. When growing any tomatoes in containers, use a soilless medium and check daily to see if they need to be watered. Fertilize all tomatoes at planting time and again monthly until harvest. Apply mulch to tomatoes in the garden to keep the soil evenly moist and prevent blossom-end rot. Just prior to harvesting, decrease watering to prevent cracking and to encourage meatier, more flavorful tomatoes.

Determinate Tomato

(Lycopersicon lycopersicum)

55–80 Days

Tomatoes are divided into two groups: determinate and indeterminate. Determinate tomatoes are bushy plants that stop growing when they reach full size. All of their fruits ripen at about the same time; the plants bear only one crop of fruit. Most pear and plum tomatoes, *L. l.* var. *pyriforme* (Roma VF Plum is pictured), are determinate; they are used for canning, sauce, and juice. Most of the dwarf varieties suitable for containers are also determinate.

GROWING TIPS

It is best to grow tomatoes from plants (either purchase them or start them indoors). Sow seeds directly in the garden only where the growing season is very long; germination rate is not as high as with seeds started indoors. Set plants in the garden after all danger of frost has passed and the soil is warm. Space determinate tomatoes 24 inches apart; they do not need to be staked. See Cherry Tomato for watering instructions. Pick the fruit as soon as it ripens.

Indeterminate Tomato
(Lycopersicon lycopersicum)

55–80 Days

Indeterminate tomatoes are vines that continue to grow, flower, and set fruit until killed by frost. Fruit from this type is used mostly for slicing and salads. Look for hybrids that are resistant to diseases. The variety Early Girl is pictured.

GROWING TIPS

Indeterminate tomatoes are cultivated in the same way as determinate tomatoes. All tomatoes prefer rich, evenly moist, slightly acid to neutral soil that is well drained. Indeterminate tomatoes can be grown in several ways. If left to grow on the ground (spaced 4 feet apart), they will produce more fruit, but the fruit will be smaller and ripen more slowly and may be prey to slugs. If pruned to 1 stem and grown on a stake or trellis (spaced 18 inches apart) they will have less fruit, but the fruit will be larger and will ripen early. Tomatoes grown in cages (spaced 2½–3 feet apart) will yield results somewhere in between. Pick tomatoes as soon as they ripen. In late fall, pick green tomatoes just before frost and let them ripen on a windowsill.

Turnip *(Brassica rapa,* Rapifera Group)

70 Days

Turnips are biennials but are grown as annuals. Both the roots and the leaves may be eaten. The roots have white, white and purple, or yellow flesh. The variety Snowball is pictured. Under favorable conditions, turnips may reach 2–3 pounds.

Growing Tips

Turnips are a cool-weather crop. Although they can be grown in spring, they grow best as a fall crop. Plant seeds in late summer or early fall, ½ inch deep in rows 8 inches apart. Thin seedlings to 3–5 inches apart. Turnips thrive in moist, rich, well-drained soil. Harvest the roots as needed once they are 2–3 inches in diameter. If you want to grow turnips in spring, prepare the soil the previous fall so seeds can be sown as early as possible. Roots will become stringy if they are not harvested before temperatures reach 80° F.

Turnip Greens *(Brassica rapa,* Rapifera Group) 45 Days

Turnip greens can be harvested and cooked as a vegetable. The rough-textured, medium green leaves are tender when young and can be harvested in a little more than half the time it takes for plants to produce usable roots. Any turnip can be used for greens; there are also hybrids grown only for greens. Purple Top White Globe is pictured.

GROWING TIPS

Turnip greens are grown in the same way as turnip roots. Since they mature quickly, they can be grown as a spring or fall crop. Sow seeds ½ inch deep and 2 inches apart. Thin the seedlings as they grow, using the thinnings as greens also. To harvest the leaves of mature plants, cut off the tops 3–4 inches above the soil line. If you want greens and roots from the same crop, take care not to damage the growing tip when you harvest the greens; the plants will produce new greens and the roots will continue to grow.

Watercress *(Nasturtium officinale)*

Watercress is an aquatic plant that has small, round green leaves with a pungent, peppery flavor. The flowers, which appear in spring, look like tiny nasturtiums. Watercress is a hardy perennial.

GROWING TIPS

Watercress must be grown in running water in full sun or in moist soil in light shade. Move seeds or plants into the garden in early spring. Young seedlings can be held in place with small stones until they become established. Space plants 8–12 inches apart. Watercress grown in soil must have fertile, sandy, neutral soil that is well drained. Harvest plants anytime when they are not in bloom by cutting back the stems. Watercress can become very weedy and may need annual thinning.

APPENDICES

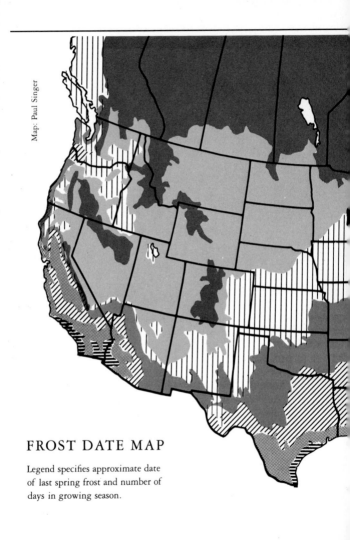

FROST DATE MAP

Legend specifies approximate date of last spring frost and number of days in growing season.

Map: Paul Singer

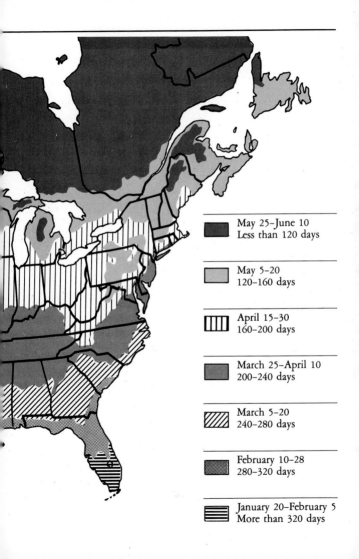

May 25–June 10
Less than 120 days

May 5–20
120–160 days

April 15–30
160–200 days

March 25–April 10
200–240 days

March 5–20
240–280 days

February 10–28
280–320 days

January 20–February 5
More than 320 days

GARDEN PESTS AND DISEASES

PLANT PESTS and diseases are a fact of life for a gardener. Therefore, it is helpful to become familiar with common pests and diseases in your area and to learn how to control them.

Symptoms of Plant Problems

Because the same general symptoms are associated with many diseases and pests, some experience is needed to determine their causes.

Diseases

Both fungi and bacteria are responsible for a variety of diseases ranging from leaf spots and wilts to root rot, but bacterial diseases usually make the affected plant tissues appear wetter than fungi do. Diseases caused by viruses and mycoplasma, often transmitted by aphids and leafhoppers, display such symptoms as mottled yellow or deformed leaves and twisted or stunted growth.

Insect Pests

Numerous insects attack plants. Sap-sucking insects—including aphids, leafhoppers, whiteflies, and scale insects—suck plant juices. The affected plant becomes yellow, stunted, and misshapen. Aphids and scale insects produce honeydew, a sticky substance that attracts ants and sooty mold fungus growth. Other pests with rasping-sucking mouthparts, such as thrips and spider mites, scrape plant tissue and then suck the juices that well up in the injured areas.

Leaf-chewers, namely beetles and caterpillars, consume plant leaves, whole or in part. Leaf miners make tunnels within the leaves, creating brown trails and causing leaf tissue to dry. In contrast, borers tunnel into shoots and stems, and their young larvae consume plant tissue, weakening the plant. Some insects, such as various grubs and maggots, feed on roots, weakening or killing the plant.

Nematodes and Cutworms

Microscopic roundworms called nematodes are other pests that attack roots and cause stunting and poor plant growth. Some kinds of nematodes produce galls on roots, while others produce them on leaves. Cutworms are moth larvae that feed near the soil line, cutting off the stems of new plants.

Snails and Slugs

Unfortunately, snails and slugs like fresh vegetables as much as we do. They usually hide underground or in mulch or debris during the day and feed at night. There are several ways to get rid of them: Go out at night and pick them off by hand; sink saucers of beer up to their rims in the dirt; save the skins of grapefruit halves and invert them in the garden, checking for the pests every morning; or use bait or traps, available at garden centers.

Environmental Stresses

Some types of plant illness result from environment-related stress, such as severe wind, drought, flooding, or extreme cold. Other problems are caused by salt toxicity, rodents, birds, nutritional deficiencies or excesses, fertilizer burn, pesticides, or damage from lawn mowers. Many of these injuries are avoidable if you take proper precautions.

Controlling Plant Problems

Always buy healthy disease- and insect-free plants. Be sure to select varieties that are disease-resistant; ask your local Cooperative Extension Service for the varieties recommended for your area. When you buy plants, check leaves and stems for dead areas or off-color and stunted tissue. Before you plant your vegetables, be sure to prepare the soil properly.

Routine Preventives

By cultivating the soil routinely you will expose insects and disease-causing organisms to the sun and thus lessen their chances of surviving in your garden. In the fall be sure to destroy infested or diseased plants, remove dead leaves and flowers, and clean up plant debris. Do not add diseased or infested material to the compost pile. Spray plants with water from time to time to dislodge insect pests and remove suffocating dust. Pick off the larger insects by hand. Buy protective collars to place at the base of seedlings to ward off cutworms. To discourage fungal leaf spots and blights, always water plants in the morning and allow the leaves to dry off before nightfall. For the same reason, provide adequate air circulation by spacing plants properly.

Weeds provide a home for insects and diseases, so pull them up or use pre-emergent herbicides (we do not recommend the use of any other type). If you use weed-killers on your lawn, do not apply them too close to your vegetable garden.

Insecticides and Fungicides

To protect plant tissue from injury due to insects and diseases, a number of insecticides and fungicides are available. However, few products control diseases due to bacteria, viruses, and mycoplasma. Pesticides are usually either "protectant" or "systemic" in nature. Protectants keep insects or disease organisms away from uninfected foliage, while systemics move through the plant and provide some therapeutic or eradicant action as well as protection. Botanical insecticides such as pyrethrum and rotenone have a shorter residual effect on pests, but are considered less toxic and generally safer for the user and the environment than inorganic chemical insecticides. Biological control through the use of ladybugs, or organisms like *Bacillus thuringiensis* (a bacterium toxic to moth and butterfly larvae), is effective and safe.

Recommended pesticides may vary to some extent from region to region. Consult your local Cooperative Extension Service or plant professional regarding the appropriate material to use. Always check the pesticide label to be sure that it is registered for use on the pest with which you are dealing and is safe for use on edible plants. Follow the label concerning safety precautions, dosage, frequency of application, and the preharvest interval—the period to wait between spraying a pesticide on food and harvesting.

ALTERNATIVE
GARDENING METHODS

THE TWO ESSAYS that follow address some optional methods of raising produce for those gardeners who want to make the most use of the space they have. Intensive gardening means using common sense practices to grow more in less space. Container gardening is an option for those gardeners who don't have room for a vegetable plot.

Intensive Gardening

Intensive gardening means growing more vegetables in less space. Once you have the experience of several successful gardening seasons, try designing your plantings for greater yield. Here are a few tips on how to accomplish this: Plan the garden's layout and seasons in great detail. Prepare the soil properly and use raised beds to add growing space. Plant disease-resistant varieties and set them as close together as the variety can stand (but not so close as to cause deformities). Plant small vegetables in blocks instead of rows. Whenever possible, train plants to grow vertically to make more use of your ground space. Harvest crops promptly and practice succession planting (replanting as soon as a crop is harvested).

Gardening in Containers

Almost any vegetable can be grown in a container; the trick is choosing types that will produce enough in a small space to be worthwhile. Small, fast-maturing greens, such as leaf lettuce, kale, Swiss chard, and mustard greens, are good choices, as are root vegetables that will grow close together (radishes, scallions, baby carrots). You can grow many fruiting vegetables in pots: tomatoes, peppers, eggplants, summer squash, and even some of the muskmelon hybrids with compact vines. There are midget and miniature varieties of many vegetables, and hybrids bred especially for containers, but they are often less productive than their full-sized relatives.

Select a container whose size is in proportion to the spread of the vegetable you will be growing in it; it must have drainage holes. Plant the vegetables in a soilless medium of peat moss with perlite or vermiculite, and keep it evenly moist. This may mean daily watering, depending on the temperature and the wind. Rotate the containers if they do not receive even sunlight. Fertilizers leach quickly from containers, so fertilize frequently (every 7 to 14 days) with soluble plant food.

VEGETABLE VARIETIES

SEED COMPANIES and plant breeders are constantly "inventing" new vegetables, which are called varieties. Some of these differ in color or shape from the old standards, while others are not visibly different but have been bred to resist certain diseases, taste better, mature quickly, or survive difficult growing conditions. Here is a brief list of some recommended varieties of the more popular vegetables.

Bean	*Green Bush:* Blue Lake, Cherokee Wax, Tender Green *Green Pole:* Blue Lake, Kentucky Wonder *Lima Bush:* Fordhook 242 *Lima Pole:* King of the Garden, Prizetaker
Beet	Burpee's Golden, Detroit Dark Red
Broccoli	Early Emerald, Green Comet, Premium Crop
Cabbage	Early Jersey Wakefield, Red Acre, Savoy Ace
Carrot	*Short:* Goldinhart, Little Finger, Short 'n' Sweet *Long:* Danvers Half-long, Nantes, Royal Chantenay, Tendersweet
Cauliflower	Early White, Royal Purple, Snow Crown

Corn   Butter and Sugar, Golden Cross Bantam, How Sweet It Is, Polar Vee, Silver Queen, Super Sweet

Cucumber   *Pickling:* County Fair 87, Earlipick, Saladin
Slicing: Bush Crop, Salad Bush, Slicemaster, Sweet Slice, Victory

Lettuce   *Butterhead:* Bibb, Buttercrunch, Dark Green Boston
Crisphead: Great Lakes, Iceberg
Leaf: Black Seeded Simpson, Grand Rapids, Red Sails, Red Salad Bowl
Romaine: Parris Island Cos

Melon   *Muskmelon:* Bush Star, Sweet 'n' Early
Watermelon: Black Diamond, Bush Jubilee, Charleston Gray, Sugar Baby

Onion   *Long-Day:* Early Yellow Globe, White Sweet Spanish, Yellow Sweet Spanish
Short-Day: Bermuda, Granex, Italian Red

Pea   *Green:* Green Arrow, Little Marvel, Maestro, Novella, Wando
Edible-podded: Oregon Sugar Pod, Sugar Daddy, Sugar Snap

Pepper   *Sweet:* Bell Boy, Better Belle, California Wonder, Gypsy, Purple Belle
Hot: Anaheim, Jalapa, Mexibell, Red Cherry Hot, Super Chili

Potato	*Baking:* Katahdin, Kennebec, Russet Burbank, White Cobbler *Red:* Explorer, Red LaSoda, Red Pontiac
Pumpkin	*Standard:* Cinderella, Connecticut Field, Jack-O'-Lantern, Spirit *Jumbo:* Big Max Mammoth
Radish	*Spring:* Cherry Belle, Easter Egg, French Breakfast, White Icicle *Winter:* Chinese White, Round Black Spanish
Squash	*Acorn:* Table Ace, Table King *Butternut:* Butterbush, Waltham *Crookneck:* Golden Summer, Sundance *Hubbard:* Blue Hubbard *Scallop:* Peter Pan, Scallopini, Sunburst *Straightneck:* Butterstick, Early Prolific *Zucchini:* Gold Rush, Gourmet Globe
Tomato	*Cherry:* Basket King, Pixie, Red Cherry, Sweet 100, Tiny Tim *Determinate:* Celebrity VFFNT, Floramerica VFF, La Roma VFF, Mamma Mia VFF, Roma VF, The Juice VF *Indeterminate:* Beefmaster VFN, Beefsteak, Better Boy VFN, Champion VFNT, Early Girl V, Lemon Boy VFN, Whopper VFNT
Turnip	All Top, Purple Top White Globe

GLOSSARY

Acid soil
Soil with a pH value lower than 7.

Alkaline soil
Soil with a pH value of more than 7.

Annual
A plant whose entire life span, from sprouting to flowering and producing seeds, is encompassed in a single growing season.

Axil
The angle between a leafstalk and the stem from which it grows.

Basal leaf
A leaf at the base of a stem.

Biennial
A plant whose life span extends to two growing seasons, sprouting in the first growing season and then flowering, producing seed, and dying in the second.

Bolting
The premature or unwanted production of flowers and seeds, often caused by excessive heat.

Bract
A modified and often scalelike leaf, usually located at the base of a flower, a fruit, or a cluster of flowers or fruits.

Bud
A young and undeveloped leaf, flower, or shoot, usually covered tightly with scales.

Bulb
A short underground stem, the swollen portion consisting mostly of fleshy, food-storing scale leaves.

Compost
A blend of decomposed organic matter not yet reduced to humus; soil or sand are sometimes added.

Compound leaf
A leaf made up of two or more leaflets.

Corm
A solid underground stem, resembling a bulb but lacking scales; often with a membranous coat.

Creeping
Prostrate or trailing over the ground or over other plants.

Crop rotation
The planting of different species in succession in one given area to reduce the risk of soilborne plant disease.

Cross-pollination
The transfer of pollen from one plant to another.

Crown
That part of a plant between the roots and the stem, usually at soil level.

Cultivar
An unvarying plant variety, maintained by vegetative propagation or by inbred seed.

Cutting
A piece of plant without roots; set in a rooting medium, it develops roots and is then potted as a new plant.

Division
Propagation by division of crowns, roots, or tubers into segments that can be induced to send out roots.

Fruit
The mature, fully developed ovary of a flower, containing one or more seeds.

Genus
A group of closely related species; plural, genera.

Germinate
To sprout.

Herb
A plant without a permanent, woody stem, usually dying back during cold weather.

Herbaceous perennial
An herb that dies back each fall, but sends out new shoots and flowers for several successive years.

Horticulture
The cultivation of plants for ornament or food.

Humus
Partly or wholly decomposed vegetable matter; an important constituent of garden soil.

Hybrid
A plant resulting from a cross between two parent plants belonging to different species, subspecies, or genera.

Invasive
Aggressively spreading from the site of cultivation.

Leaflet
One of the subdivisions of a compound leaf.

Legume
A member of the pea and bean family, whose fruits are pods that split in half and have the seeds attached to the lower seam.

Loam
A humus-rich soil containing up to 25 percent clay, up to 50 percent silt, and less than 50 percent sand.

Margin
The edge of a leaf.

Mulch
A protective covering spread over the soil around the base of plants to retard evaporation, control temperature, or enrich the soil.

Neutral soil
Soil that is neither acid nor alkaline, having a pH value of 7.

Node
The place on the stem where leaves or branches are attached.

Peat moss
Partly decomposed moss, rich in nutrients and with a high water retention, used as a component of garden soil.

Perennial
A plant whose life span extends over several growing seasons and that produces seeds in several growing seasons.

pH
A symbol for the hydrogen ion content of the soil, and thus a means of expressing the acidity or alkalinity of the soil.

Pollen
Minute grains containing the male germ cells and released by the stamens.

Propagate
To produce new plants, either by vegetative means involving the rooting of pieces of a plant, or by sowing seeds.

Rhizome
A horizontal underground stem, distinguished from a root by the presence of nodes and often enlarged by food storage.

Rosette
A crowded cluster of leaves; usually basal, circular, and at ground level.

Runner
A prostrate shoot, rooting at its nodes.

Seed
A fertilized, ripened ovule, almost always covered with a protective coating and contained in a fruit.

Species
A population of plants or animals whose members are at least potentially able to breed with each other, but which is reproductively isolated from other populations.

Succession planting
The planting of one garden crop directly after the harvest of another to increase the yield of a given area during one growing season.

Succulent
A plant with thick fleshy leaves or stems that contain abundant water-storage tissues.

Taproot
The main, central root of a plant.

Terminal
Borne at the tip of a stem or shoot, rather than in the axil.

Till
To work the soil into small fragments.

Toothed
Having the margin shallowly divided into small, toothlike segments.

Tuber
A swollen, mostly underground stem that bears buds and serves as a storage site for food.

Tufted
Growing in dense clumps, cushions, or tufts.

Variety
A population of plants that differs consistently from the typical form of the species, either occurring naturally or produced in cultivation.

Vegetative propagation
Propagation by means other than seed.

Whorl
A group of three or more leaves or shoots, all emerging from a stem at a single node.

PHOTO CREDITS

INDEX

Abelmoschus esculentus, 65

Allium
  ampeloprasum, Porrum Group, 56
  cepa, 85
  cepa, Aggregatum Group, 86
  cepa, Cepa Group, 66, 67
  fistulosum, 85
  sativum, 50

Apium
  graveolens var. *dulce,* 41
  graveolens var. *rapaceum,* 40

Arachis hypogaea, 72

Armoracia rusticana, 52

Artichoke, 26

Arugula, 27

Asparagus, 28

Asparagus officinalis, 28

Aubergine, 47

Bean
  Blue Lake Snap, 31
  Broad, 29
  Fava, 29
  Fordhook 242 Lima, 30
  Lima, 30
  Snap, 31
  String, 31

Beet, 32

Beta
  vulgaris, Cicla Group, 98

  vulgaris, Crassa Group, 32

Bok Choy, 36

Brassica
  juncea, 64
  napus, Napobrassica Group, 83
  oleracea, Acephala Group, 43, 54
  oleracea, Botrytis Group, 33, 39
  oleracea, Capitata Group, 35
  oleracea, Gemmifera Group, 34
  oleracea, Gongylodes Group, 55
  rapa, Chinensis Group, 36
  rapa, Rapifera Group, 102, 103

Broccoli, 33
  Early Emerald, 33

Brussels Sprouts, 34

Cabbage, 35
  Chinese, 36
  Early Jersey Wakefield, 35
  Red, 35
  Savoy, 35

Cantaloupe, 62

Cape Gooseberry, 37
  Dwarf, 37

Capsicum
  annuum, 73, 74
  frutescens, 73

Carrot, 38
  Royal Chantenay, 38

Cauliflower, 39

Purple Head, 39
Celeriac, 40
Celery, 41
 Knob, 40
 Turnip-rooted, 40
Celery Mustard, 36
Chicory
 Leaf, 42, 79
 Magdeburg, 42
 Pain de Sucre Leaf, 42
Cichorium
 endiva, 48
 intybus, 42, 79
Citrullus lanatus, 63
Collards, 43
Corn, Sweet, 44
Cucumber, 45
 Liberty Pickling, 46
 Pickling, 46
Cucumis
 melo, Inodorus Group, 61
 melo, Reticulatus Group, 62
 sativus, 45, 46
Cucurbita, 78
 maxima, 78, 92
 moschata, 90
 pepo, 78, 89, 91, 93, 94, 95
Cynara scolymus, 26

Daikon, 81
Daucus carota var. *sativus*, 38

Eggplant, 47
 Black Beauty, 47
Endive, Curly, 48

Eruca vesicaria sativa, 27
Escarole, 48

Fennel, Florence, 49
Finocchio, 49
Foeniculum vulgare var. *azoricum*, 49
Fragaria × *ananassa*, 96

Garlic, 50
Ginger, 51

Helianthus
 annuus, 97
 tuberosus, 53
Horseradish, 52
Husk Tomato, Ground, 37

Ipomoea batatas, 77

Jerusalem Artichoke, 53

Kale, 54
Kohlrabi, 55

Lactuca sativa, 57, 58, 59, 60
Leek, 56
Lettuce
 Bibb Butterhead, 57
 Buttercrunch, 57
 Butterhead, 57
 Cos, 60
 Crisphead, 58
 Great Lakes Crisphead, 58
 Iceberg, 58
 Leaf, 59

Paris White Cos, 60
Red Salad Bowl Leaf, 59
Romaine, 60
Lycopersicon
lycopersicum, 100, 101
lycopersicum var. *cerasiforme,* 99
lycopersicum var. *pyriforme,* 100

Melon
Casaba, 61
Crenshaw, 61
Honeydew, 61
Musk-, 62
Water-, 63
Muskmelon, 62
Sweet 'n' Early, 62
Mustard Greens, 64

Nasturtium officinale, 104

Okra, 65
Clemson Spineless, 65
Onion
Bunching, 85
Green, 85
Italian Red, 67
Long-Day, 66
Short-Day, 67
Yellow Spanish, 66

Pak-Choi, 36
Parsley
Root, 68
Turnip, 68
Parsnip, 69
Pastinaca sativa, 69

Pea
Burpee Blue Bantam, 71
Edible-Podded, 70
English, 71
Green, 71
Snow, 70
Sugar Snap, 70
Peanut, 72
Pepper
Anaheim Hot, 73
Golden California Wonder Sweet, 7
Hot, 73
Sweet, 74
Tabasco, 73
Petroselinum crispum var. *tuberosum,* 68
Phaseolus
limensis, 30
vulgaris, 31
Physalis, 37
ixocarpa, 37
peruviana, 37
pruinosa, 37
Pisum
sativum, 71
sativum var. *macrocarpon,* 70
Potato
Baking, 75
Boiling, 76
Katahdin, 75
Red LaSoda, 76
Sweet, 77
Pumpkin, 78
Big Max Mammoth, 78

Radicchio, 79
Rouge di Verona, 79

Radish
  Champion Spring, 80
  Daikon, 81
  Oriental, 81
  Spring, 80
  Winter, 81
Raphanus
  sativus, 80
  sativus var. *longipinnatus*, 81
Rheum rhabarbarum, 82
Rhubarb, 82
Rocket, 27
Roquette, 27
Rutabaga, 83

Salsify, 84
Scallion, 85
Shallot, 86
Solanum
  melongena var. *esculentum*, 47
  tuberosum, 75, 76
Spinach, 87
  Melody, 87
  New Zealand, 88
Spinacia oleracea, 87
Squash
  Acorn, 89
  Butternut, 90
  Crookneck, 91
  Early Prolific Straightneck, 94
  Hubbard, 92
  Patty Pan, 93
  Scallop, 93
  Spaghetti, 89
  Straightneck, 94

  Summer, 91, 93, 94, 95
  Turban, 92
  Winter, 89, 90, 92
  Zucchini, 95
Strawberry, 96
Sunflower, 97
Swiss Chard, 98

Tetragonia tetragonioides, 88
Tomatillo, 37
Tomato
  Cherry, 99
  Determinate, 100
  Early Girl, 101
  Indeterminate, 101
  Pear, 100
  Plum, 100
  Roma VF Plum, 100
Tragopogon porrifolius, 84
Turnip, 102
  Greens, 103
  Purple Top White Globe, 103
  Snowball, 102
  Swedish, 83

Vegetable Oyster, 84
Vicia faba, 29

Watercress, 104
Watermelon, 63
  Sugar Baby, 63

Yam, 77

Zea mays var. *rugosa*, 44
Zingiber officinale, 51
Zucchini, 95

CHANTICLEER PRESS
STEWART, TABORI & CHANG

Publisher
ANDREW STEWART

Senior Editor
ANN WHITMAN

Editor
CAROL MCKEOWN

Project Editor
AMY HUGHES

Production
KATHY ROSENBLOOM
KARYN SLUTSKY

Design
JOSEPH RUTT